THE UNOFFICIAL BOOK OF

HARVARD TRIVIA

BY DAVID J. LOFTUS

OMNIA VINCIT RISUS

Quinlan Press
Boston, Massachusetts

Copyright © by
Quinlan Press, Inc.
All rights reserved,
including the right of reproduction
in whole or in part in any form.
Published by Quinlan Press, Inc.
131 Beverly Street
Boston, MA 02114

Cover design by Tina Chomka

Library of Congress Catalog Card Number
85-62789
ISBN 0-933341-22-9

First printing November 1985

Acknowledgments

I am indebted to the people of the Harvard community for their kind and ready assistance. University Archivist Harley Holden, Photo Archivist Robin McElhenny, and the cheerful employees of the University Archives were most helpful. Jean Martin at **Harvard Magazine** and Editor Emeritus William Bentinck-Smith gave me some leads. I also received information from Rare Books curator Roger Stoddard, WHRB alumnus and advisor David Eliot, Associate Dean of Freshmen Burriss Young, and William Tobey of the News Office. Radcliffe Archivist Jane Knowles and Schlesinger librarian Eva Mosely helped me with the distaff side. Louise Ambler and Caroline Jones fed me facts from the Fogg while it was closed for renovations. I took the Crimson key tour led by Jim Sanks. I gleaned a few obscure facts with the help of Recording Secretary John Hanselman, Marion Briefer at the reunion office, Gene Arcand at the Office of Facilities, Cathleen Montague at the Faculty Club, and Tami Nason at the Harvard Management Office.

Off campus, I made use of the Cambridge Historical Commission and Cambridge Traffic engineer Loren Preston. Paul Killiam '37 graciously screened his film and slide extravaganza, "John Harvard: Movie Star," for me, and will present the show to interested Harvard Clubs and alumni gatherings. My friends John Cole '81 and Acha Lord '79 lent me their VCR and provided some really arcane facts. Brian Donaher translated my epigraph into Latin.

Thanks to the crew at Quinlan Press for putting up with my fussiness during production.

Theresa Shimer gave me her love and willingly read trashy Harvard novels when I overdosed.

PREFACE

A college with a 350-year history accumulates a considerable amount of data. In trying to select a collection of facts suitable for a book of trivia, the author had to decide what he was **not** looking for.

You will not find questions about the size of Harvard's endowment or the date of some president's installation. Such facts are important, and perhaps even interesting to a person with an odd turn of mind, but they are not appropriate fodder for this book.

For the essence of a trivial fact is that it begs to be passed on. It should bring a grin to the reader's face, perhaps a touch of astonishment, and the desire to share it with someone else. Trivia is the provender of conversation. It is doubtful that people buy a book of trivia in order to test themselves, but rather to be diverted.

With that aim in mind, rigorous efforts were made to weed out indispensable facts. The author does not claim to be infallible, however. If the reader manages to identify an inexplicably vital entry, he should alert the author posthaste.

Happily, in the life of an august institution such as Harvard, irrelevancies crop up every day. If enough additional details of a petty nature are brought to the author's attention by solicitous readers, we may generate a second volume of Harvard trivia.

In the meantime, enjoy!

Table of Contents

HISTORY, PART I
   QUESTIONS 1
   ANSWERS 133

ALUMNI
   QUESTIONS 7
   ANSWERS 137

HARVARD IN FICTION
   QUESTIONS 19
   ANSWERS 143

BUILDINGS & GROUNDS
   QUESTIONS 27
   ANSWERS 147

ASSESSMENTS OF THE COLLEGE AND ITS MEN
   QUESTIONS 33
   ANSWERS 153

HISTORY, PART II
   QUESTIONS 39
   ANSWERS 155

SPORTS
   QUESTIONS 45
   ANSWERS 159

HARVARD IN FILMS
   QUESTIONS 59
   ANSWERS 171

STUDENT LIFE
   QUESTIONS 65
   ANSWERS 175

THE WOMEN
　　QUESTIONS 71
　　ANSWERS 179

SCHOOL DAYS
　　QUESTIONS 79
　　ANSWERS 183

DROPOUTS & SPECIAL STUDENTS
　　QUESTIONS 93
　　ANSWERS 189

PHOTOGRAPHS
　　QUESTIONS 99
　　ANSWERS 193

MISCELLANY
　　QUESTIONS 121
　　ANSWERS 199

QUESTIONS

HISTORY
PART I

1. In his book **John Harvard and His Times,** Henry C. Shelley labored to prove that what famous personage had introduced John Harvard's parents to each other?

2. After he decided to emigrate to the Massachusetts Bay Colony, John Harvard set about purchasing a large quantity of _____.

3. What was the name of the town where —on November 16, 1637—the General Court of Massachusetts stated its intention to erect a college?

4. True or False: This town was the capital of the Massachusetts Bay Colony.

5. At what other location could the new college have been located?

6. The Pequot Indian Wars were partly responsible for delaying the opening of the college. Another distraction was the person who asserted the people of the

History I

Commonwealth could communicate with God without the assistance of ministers trained at a "Ninneversity," as a follower put it. Who was this rabble-rouser?

7. If you know the answers to the following questions, then you know how tenuous is the connection between John Harvard and the school that bears his name.
   a) Where was John Harvard when the college was founded?
   b) How many years did he live in the Massachusetts Bay Colony?
   c) Did he make his bequest to the college in writing?
   d) How long had the college been open when he died?

8. Which is older, Harvard College or Boston Latin School?

9. How many books did John Harvard leave the college?

10. How many books from John Harvard's library exist today?

11. How many years passed after the founding of the college before a man named Harvard graduated from it?

12. Which two of the following works did not appear in John Harvard's collection?
    a) Descartes, **Discours sur la Methode**
    b) Pliny the Younger, **Historie of the World**
    c) Terence, **Comoediae sex**
    d) Bacon, **A Natural History**
    e) Shakespeare, **First Folio**
    f) Aesop, **Fables**

History I

13. The first master of Harvard College, the Reverend Nathaniel Eaton, was fired by the General Court after only one year. Why?

14. Reverend Eaton's wife scandalized the Court by admitting she had never served the students beef and sometimes allowed a week to ten days to pass between servings of beer, but she denied the accusations made about her mackerel and hasty pudding. What was said to be wrong with them?

15. How did the first master of Harvard College end his days?

16. Eaton's successor was Henry Dunster, the first president of Harvard College. He was paid only sporadically for his services, yet he managed to survive in the job for fourteen years. What was the primary source of support that got him through?

17. For 107 years, from 1640 to 1747, Harvard College derived its only dependable annual income from what local source of transportation?

18. In what year did the first Harvard class graduate?

19. How many graduates were in the first class?

20. In December 1643, a college seal with three books carrying the word "Veritas" was chosen by the Board of Overseers. How soon did this device appear in public?

History I

21. In the interest of medical studies, the General Court promised in 1647 to give Harvard something at least once every four years. What object did they promise to furnish?

22. In 1653 various local towns agreed to collect an annual levy to support the college. The town of Salem, which might have been host to Harvard if the college had located on the Marblehead plot the town had offered in 1637, held a meeting which about fifty people attended. What happened?

23. Why were there two classes of 1653?

24. Which one of the following items was **not** used by the first Harvard students as partial payment for their tuition, at least according to college records as reported by Samuel Eliot Morison?
    a) wheat
    b) oxen
    c) spices
    d) turnips
    e) honey
    f) rose water
    g) joint stools
    h) ribbon
    i) shoes
    j) malt
    k) salt beef
    l) apples
    m) firewood
    n) sack (for imbibing, not for carrying)
    o) canvas
    p) silk
    q) a sword

25. President Dunster was once called back to the college from a social visit in Concord on urgent business. He solemnly emptied his horn of gunpowder in a trail through the Yard and touched it off with a live coal. What was he doing?

26. In what form was the salary of the first Harvard presidents usually paid?

History I

27. Harvard did not issue diplomas to its graduating classes for _____.
    a) ten years
    b) more than half its history
    c) one hundred and twenty years
    d) sixty years

28. Why was President Dunster compelled to resign after fourteen years of tireless service?

29. According to the laws of the college, what was one of the president's primary on-campus duties in the 17th century?

30. Stoughton Hall is named for William Stoughton, AB 1654, a Massachusetts governor and chief justice. For what role is he infamous?

31. What is Caleb Cheeshahteaumuck's significance in Harvard history?

32. No papers of Harvard's second president, Charles Chauncy, have survived to this day, but we know what happened to them. How were they destroyed?

33. What was **Mamusse Wunneetupanatamwe Up-Bidum God**?

34. Under President Chauncy, the college press prepared a translation of a notable book until the General Court of Massachusetts passed a resolution preventing the publication of the volume, "wherein is conteyned some things that are unsafe for the people of this place." What is the name of the book?

History I

35. Enrollment fell during the uninspiring administration of President Chauncy. How many students graduated in 1672, the year that he died?

ALUMNI

1. What member of the class of 1743, perhaps the American Revolution's most brilliant orator, was killed by a bolt of lightning in 1783?

2. In the 1920s, the days of debunking biographies, Herbert Mayes composed **A Biography Without a Hero**, an utter fabrication which asserted that a Harvard graduate of the class of 1852 had had a penchant for high living, a schizoid personality, and innumerable love affairs. Other serious writers, including the compilers of the **Dictionary of American Biography**, were taken in by this scurrilous account of one of the best-selling authors in American history. Who was the maligned subject?

3. In his tenth anniversary class report, this graduate said he was an economist at the RAND Corporation. In his fifteenth, written while he was in a Bangkok nursing home with hepatitis, he wrote eloquently of his inability to decide whether to stay on in the government of Vietnam or return home to research and con-

Alumni

sulting. His twenty-fifth anniversary report noted his recent trial for thirteen counts of violations of federal espionage, theft, and conspiracy statutes, and he thanked all the classmates who had contributed to his defense fund. What is his name?

4. What member of the class of 1936 accidentally shot and killed his wife in 1951, reportedly while playing William Tell and trying to shoot a champagne glass off her head?

5. John Updike has said more than once that his true ambition was to be a _____.

6. What member of the class of 1924 resigned his seat in the U.S. Senate early in 1944 to enter active military service?

7. What 1958 graduate co-authored the screenplay for the Beatles animated feature **The Yellow Submarine**?

8. As his 25th Class Report notes, **The New York Times** called his books classics, and more than one reviewer has called him America's number-one social historian; on the other hand, one newspaper called him "a non-book writer of non-history of non-existent Society." Who is this 1939 graduate?

9. What Harvard graduate wrote in his 25th Class Report, "I've spent all these years reporting a series of history-makers that started with Chou-En-lai in China in 1939 and continues to John F.

Kennedy in Washington in 1962; and I still don't know what makes history go." What's his name?

10. Norman Mailer '43 wrote that a member of the class of 1936 was perhaps "the only American novelist living today who may conceivably be possessed by genius." Whom was he touting?

11. After working for the Atomic Energy Commission plant at Los Alamos, this fellow issued his first record album on a privately manufactured LP in 1953. He made 400 copies for $15, and the record eventually sold 350,000 copies. What is his name?

12. A member of the class of 1971, this musician joined a trio that had been playing at CBGB in New York with Television and the Ramones, just in time for their first album in 1977, which sold 100,000 copies. Who is he?

13. Highly impressed with a singer he met in Detroit, Tom Rush began to perform some of her songs. He recorded a demo tape of her composition "Urge For Going" and sent it over to WBZ. As soon as the station put it on the air, it shot to number one on its request list, but Elektra Records did not press it for a year and a half, when it was too late. But Rush had helped to launch the career of the song's composer. What is her name?

14. In a review of **Self-Portrait in a Convex Mirror**, which was eventually to win the

Alumni

National Book Award, the Pulitzer Prize and the National Book Critics Circle Award, William Pritchard wrote that the author—a member of the class of 1949 —"is too much the kind of writer that makes Gerald Ford or Scoop Jackson feel good about not reading poetry." What is the poet's name?

15. Which Harvard graduate read briefly from his works on "Saturday Night Live" in November 1981?

16. Who replaced the ailing Bruno Walter to conduct the New York Philharmonic on a Sunday afternoon in 1943, when he was only twenty-five years old?

17. Jeffery Hudson, John Lange, and Michael Douglas are all pseudonyms for what '64 graduate?

18. What respected scholar was born in Huron, South Dakota, and attended Phillips Exeter and the University of Wisconsin before getting his undergraduate degree at Harvard in 1929?

19. What journalist, reporting from Warsaw in 1965-66, earned the official disapproval of the Polish Foreign Ministry for his pieces and was expelled from the country?

20. The most recent biographer of this alumnus found evidence that his subject left his ministry at the First Unitarian Parish of Brewster on Cape Cod because several young boys in the congregation had informed their parents of

Alumni

sexual molestation. The banished shepherd went on to write such books as **Luck and Pluck**, **Ragged Dick**, and **From Farm Boy to Senator**. Who is he?

21. Which one of the following activities has William Burroughs **not** pursued?
    a) Employment at a New York advertising firm
    b) Marijuana farming in Texas
    c) Graduate study in Aztec and Mayan archaeology at Mexico City University
    d) Service in the Office of Strategic Services
    e) Pest extermination
    f) Private investigation
    g) Service in the U.S. Army
    h) Graduate study in anthropology at Harvard

22. This '39 alumnus has played a prominent role in saving endangered animals, hauling 580 wild burros from the floor of the Grand Canyon in 1981 and 308 Andalusian goats from the U.S. Navy-owned San Clemente Island off San Diego. "It would be such a rotten world if everything in it had only two legs," he has said. Who is he?

23. After graduating from Harvard Medical School, this man was a post-doctoral fellow at the Salk Institute for Biological Studies in La Jolla, California. At least that's what they decided to call him: "Part of my deal with them was that I would not have to go to the lab." Who is this person, and what was he really doing at the Salk Institute?

24. Until his mid teens, this '52 alumnus trained to be a concert pianist, "you

Alumni

know, practicing four hours a day, twelve hours on Saturday." When his mother died, he thought, now I don't have to be a concert pianist. What's his name?

25. What respected doctor published a novel about a Jewish candidate for U.S. president, **The Wanting of Levine**, in 1978?

26. **The Off-Islanders**, a novel by Nathaniel Benchley '38, was the basis for what film?

27. George Burroughs, AB 1670, is notable for what reason?

28. What Harvard graduate went to London in 1780 to study painting under Benjamin West and was arrested as a spy, imprisoned for nearly eight months, and then deported, only to sneak back later to continue his tutelage?

29. Stephen Hanan '68 was uniquely gifted to help composer Andrew Lloyd Webber in what way?

30. What two Harvard graduates starred almost entirely alone together in a 1981 cult classic film, the first film in which either had ever appeared?

31. What member of the very first Harvard class managed to stay in power under both the Cromwells **and** Charles II, and what famous address carries his name?

32. What 1800 graduate was called "the first genius produced by the western world"

Alumni

by Coleridge, and had a town in greater Boston named after him?

33. Hughes Mearns, AB 1902, is not nearly as well known as a little poem he wrote called "Antigonish." Can you recite the poem?

34. William Burroughs collaborated with Jack Kerouac on a novel in 1944. The two men wrote alternating chapters in Dashiell Hammett style about a murder based on an actual case in which both had been detained as material witnesses. The novel was never published. What is its name?

35. Where did Michael Crichton get the pseudonym "Jeffery Hudson"?

36. This 1950 alumnus was giving a poetry reading when Jack Kerouac interrupted with the words, "You're ruining American poetry!" Our man replied, "That's more than you could ever do!" Who was he?

37. Which 1950 graduate has published under the pseudonyms Eduard Blutig, Mrs. Regera Dowdy, Dreary Wodge, Drew Dogyear, Roy Grewdead, and Raddory Gewe?

38. Robert E. Sherwood's first job in films came in 1924 when he was paid $2,500 to rewrite the subtitles for what silent classic?

39. Which 1927 alumnus designed New York City's Seagram Building with Mies

Alumni

Van Der Rohe in 1956, and Lincoln Center in 1964?

40. This composer's works include the ballets "Filling Station" and "Bayou," a piece called "The Courtship of Yongly Bongly Bo," and an arrangement of "Bugles and Birds," based on the original score by Pablo Picasso. What is the composer's name?

41. What WHRB alumnus was based in Israel with CBS-TV until he flew to Rome to report a story the Israeli authorities would not allow out of the country, and was barred from reentering Israel?

42. What Harvard graduate made his film debut as a Bedouin extra in **Lawrence of Arabia**, played a bad guy shot by John Wayne in **Rio Lobo**, and fought in a bullfight staged by Hemingway in 1954?

43. What 1931 graduate studied chemistry in college, clerked for U.S. Supreme Court Justice Brandeis, and ended up a professor of sociology at his alma mater?

44. Film critic and amateur etymologist John Simon '46 is a native of what country?

45. Pedro Albizu y Campos '16 was heavily involved in Nationalist activities in his native Puerto Rico. In October 1950 police surrounded his home and routed him with tear gas because of his role in an attempt on the life of _____.

Alumni

46. What 1909 graduate entered Harvard as a special student at age twenty-seven and eventually became a radio journalist who interviewed Hitler and Mussolini?

47. The author of verses such as "Poem (Lana Turner has collapsed!)" received recognition partly because of his early and meaningless death at age forty. How did he die?

48. What Harvard man has a flowing white beard and habitually dresses in a large fur coat, a long ski scarf, a quail-stalker's cap, and tennis shoes?

49. What 1948 graduate once said, "If I wanted to be President, which of course I don't, I'd still **rather** be George Plimpton"?

50. Joe Raposo '58 composed music for what popular television show?

51. Who published a book of wartime poems called **Rhymes of a PFC**?

52. What Harvard graduate introduced a character in the novel **No Hero** upon whom a popular series of motion pictures starring Peter Lorre was based?

53. Who played Big Frenchy Demange, best friend and bodyguard to the owner of **The Cotton Club**?

54. What Harvard graduate headed the Office of Management and Budget, chaired the Atomic Energy Commission, directed the CIA, and served as Secretary of Energy and of Defense?

Alumni

55. E.L. Thayer, AB 1885, wrote verse for Hearst's **San Francisco Examiner**. What is his most famous composition?

56. Accredited as a correspondent for Father Charles Coughlin's **Social Justice**, this Harvard man shared a room with William L. Shirer on a press junket in occupied Poland. Soon after, Shirer's best-selling **Berlin Diary** called him "an American Fascist" and went on to say, "None of us can stand the fellow and suspect he is spying on us for the Nazis...." Who is he?

57. Fresh out of the Navy, this '42 grad decided at age twenty-four to take on New Hampshire publisher William Loeb by setting up a rival newspaper in Manchester. Two years later, in 1948, Loeb bought out the rival paper and fired his young rival. Who was he?

58. What Pulitzer Prize-winning journalist has a Bally machine in his home and was termed one of the two preeminent pinball players in New York City by John McPhee?

59. The first year he worked for his father's firm, this 1926 graduate personally boosted fur sales from $74,000 to $420,000. Who is he?

60. What Harvard graduate co-authored **Farewell to the Model T** with E.B. White?

61. Six U.S. presidents have been Harvard men. Most people recall the two

Roosevelts, the two Adamses, and a Kennedy, but who was the sixth?

62. Phillips Brooks, AB 1855, is the author of what popular Christmas carol?

63. Which 1969 graduate has appeared in films with Lawrence Olivier, Sissy Spacek, Faye Dunaway, and Sally Field?

64. Which future syndicate columnist (AB 1932) was an aide to General Claire Chennault, and was captured by the Japanese in Hong Kong and held until exchanged in June 1942?

65. Who wrote **Love Everybody Crusade**, **The Perfect Solution to Absolutely Everything**, and **Mr. Nixon and My Other Problems**?

66. The three men who lost their federal jobs on the night of October 20-21, 1973 all had some kind of Harvard degree. Can you name the men and the schools that gave them their Harvard shingle?

67. Which Reagan cabinet minister was a Harvard man?

68. Which 1950 graduate published a book that was illustrated by Norman Rockwell?

69. A nose gunner and bombardier with the Army Air Forces in 1944 to 1946, this 1947 graduate trained with the Special Forces and saw action in Viet Nam to

Alumni

gain background for his bestseller, which became a John Wayne movie. What is the author's name?

70. This 20th-century composer is known for the technical complexity of his compositions. The violinist for whom he composed his "Concerto For Violin" (1935) declared the piece "unplayable." Who is the composer?

71. Which 1936 graduate was probably the only Harvard man to hold a master pilot's license for navigation on the Mississippi?

72. Which 1930 alumnus won the Pulitzer for his "Third String Quartet" in 1971, a year after his alma mater gave him an honorary doctorate?

73. Which 1967 honors graduate portrayed the mad Dr. Lizardo in **The Adventures of Buckaroo Banzai Across the Eighth Dimension** and Roberta Muldoon, the transsexual football player in **The World According to Garp?**

74. What Harvard graduate published a book on Frank Sinatra in 1985?

75. In what film did Tommy Lee Jones make his screen debut?

HARVARD IN FICTION

1. In the April 1908 issue of the **Harvard Monthly**, a sophomore published a story in which the enraged narrator explodes a bomb in the office of the dean. Who is the author?

2. In what novel does a student fall into a pep rally bonfire and burn to death?

3. A conversation between freshman Quentin Compson and his roommate Shrevlin McCannon in their Harvard suite forms much of the text of what novel?

4. Quentin Compson was a member of what Harvard class?

5. In the opening pages of **The Women's Room**, a character named Mira hides in a restroom in the basement of what Harvard building?

6. Kurt Vonnegut once said, "To put down **Love Story** is like putting down a _____."

19

Fiction

7. From what novel does the following passage come?

> I admit everyone I know who's been invited to Harvard and then ignored—from Junior Fellows to the most Senior Visiting Professors—always thinks there's a conspiracy to ignore them when it's just the wonderful Harvard manner. But if they didn't want her to crack, why did they dope her and drop her in a bathtub, and then call in the women most likely to make her look horrible in her own eyes?

8. In what short story does a Harvard freshman named Henry Palamountain hitchhike to school from Oregon?

9. In which novel is the corpse of Professor Singer found in his "Hallowell House" suite?

10. In Rona Jaffe's **Class Reunion**, what building is said to look like Grand Central Station and smell like a zoo?

11. What Boston-based private investigator attended the 1982 Harvard commencement to see his girlfriend receive her Ph.D. in clinical psychology, and in what novel?

12. From what novel does the following sentence come: "We have sold Benjy's pasture so that Quentin may go to Harvard"?

13. What was the full name of Oliver's mother in **Love Story**?

14. In what Harvard building were Oliver and Jenny married?

Fiction

15. In which novel does an undergraduate named Robert Putney Drake pass in a paper to the Harvard Department of Psychology on the last words of Dutch Schultz?

16. From what state does Hart, the hero of **The Paper Chase**, hail?

17. What does Hart do with the letter that contains his first-year law school grades?

18. Which Kurt Vonnegut character attended Harvard College, interrupted his studies at Harvard Law to join the U.S. Army on December 8, 1941, and took his law degree after the war?

19. In Melville's **Moby Dick**, what was "my Yale College and my Harvard"?

20. How did Quentin Compson end his freshman year—and his affiliation with Harvard?

21. Identify the source of the following passage:

> It is not only that his affair with Wendy consumes certain hours; more profoundly, it consumes the emotional and physical energy which at other times has been sublimated into the writing of political history. As his roommate had put it once back at Harvard, when Brian made a similar choice before an important exam: "Brian thinks it all comes out of the same faucet."
> "I know it does," he replied.
> "You're nuts," said his roommate cheerfully.
> "The way I look at it, the more I screw the better I work."

Fiction

22. In which novel does Peter Fallon, a Harvard graduate student in history, discover that a silver tea set in the Boston Museum of Fine Arts attributed to Paul Revere is a fake?

23. Where does the real Revere tea set turn out to be buried?

24. In what novel does a Harvard grad student habitually hold his breath on the subway train between Harvard and Central, "with his lungs expanded to the bursting point and his chest swollen and stuck out like the breast of a pouter pigeon, while his eyes bulged, the veins on his forehead stuck out, and his face slowly turned an apoplectic purple as he sat there rocking with the agony of his effort"?

25. Which novel includes the plot device of a "Madonna" painted by the Renaissance artist Lorenzo Lotto?

26. In which novel does a Harvard English professor named Edward Cavan commit suicide by throwing himself under an elevated train?

27. The protagonists of Anton Myrer's **The Last Convertible** are members of which Harvard class?

28. In what year does George Virdon, the narrator of **The Last Convertible**, take his degree?

29. On a May morning in 1942, after receiving news of the death of Jean-Jean,

Fiction

George Virdon makes an illegal trip through campus in the beautiful car left to his care. What was wrong with his itinerary?

30. Now he would prowl the stacks of the library at night, pulling books out of a thousand shelves and reading in them like a madman. The thought of these vast stacks of books would drive him mad: the more he read, the less he seemed to know.... he would read watch in hand, muttering to himself in triumph or anger at the timing of each page: "Fifty seconds to do that one. Damn you, we'll see! You will, will you!"—and he would tear through the next page in twenty seconds.

    Who is this character, and in what novel does he try to read every book in Widener?

31. In which novel is the Harvard quarterback offered a $2,000 bribe to "throw" the Yale game at the end of an undefeated season, and what does he do?

32. Jane Langton's novel, **The Memorial Hall Murder**, set in the near but vaguely defined future, clashes with Harvard reality in a couple of ways. One important campus office is no longer located where Langton puts it, one architectural project she allows for has yet to be completed, and one Harvard official said to have vacated his post remains in office. Can you identify these discrepancies?

33. Identify the source of the following passage:
    "Look here. He's another Harvard. Went in as a Curry appointment. Don't your little personnel boys understand what we're trying to

Fiction

do, Frank? Can't we find a tough bastard who is for us? Maybe a graduate of Tulane or Kansas State or Illinois? Take this bastard off the list, Frank, and never again, **never** again bring me a name from Harvard."

34. In what novel does a Harvard undergraduate plunge down a toilet bowl after a lost harmonica?

35. What is the student's name in the novel of the previous question?

36. **Of Time and the River** includes the character of a Cambridge spinster who lives on Garden Street and holds Friday afternoon parties at which she tries to provoke arguments by seating antagonistic persons next to each other. For example, she puts Professor Lawes, author of **Sanity and Tradition in the Renaissance**, beside Mr. Wilder, who painted that picture everyone's talking about, "_____."

37. Identify the source of the following passage:
> As a Harvard undergraduate he had won prizes in scholarship for just about everything.... In short, Clevinger was one of those people with lots of intelligence and no brains, and everyone knew it except those who soon found it out....He often looked...like one of those people hanging around modern museums with both eyes together on one side of the face. It was an illusion, of course, generated by Clevinger's predilection for staring fixedly at one side of a question and never seeing the other side at all.... He was a militant idealist who crusaded against racial bigotry by growing faint in its presence.

Fiction

38. In what novel do we find an elderly woman named Miss Figwort (Radcliffe '18) trying to develop and breed a phoenix?

39. Who was the fictional 1938 graduate who landed a job as Nixon's special advisor on youth affairs and went to prison in 1975 for his role in the Watergate affair?

40. Which book of vignettes contains stories that take place at Harvard and at the Esalen Institute in Big Sur, California?

41. In which Harvard novel do two students perform well on a final because they skipped studying the preceding day to go on a mad hunt for a mysterious tavern near Quincy and stayed out all night?

42. In which novel does a Harvard senior skip off at Christmas to live in Europe for eight months with a Radcliffe girl named Wendy?

43. In **Death in a Tenured Position**, Amanda Cross retells the story of what amusing **Crimson** headline about President Lowell's opposition to subway construction just outside Harvard Yard?

44. From the writings of what Harvard graduate did George Weller take the title of his Harvard novel, **Not To Eat, Not For Love**?

45. The style of Weller's novel has often been compared to that of what more famous Harvard-educated novelist?

Fiction

46. What is the name of the Harvard novel by "Leonie St. John"?

47. In **Girl With a Zebra**, Margaret Mallet and three other "North Hollow Junior College" girls get stranded for several hours in the middle of the night in what Harvard tower?

48. What's the name of the zebra in **Girl With a Zebra**?

49. In **H.M. Pulham, Esquire**, what is the name of the New York copywriter with whom Harry Pulham '15 falls in love?

50. In which novel does Harvard appear as "Rowley College"?

51. **The Last Convertible** has a 25th reunion, **H.M. Pulham, Esquire** has a 25th reunion, and **Class Reunion** has a 20th reunion. Which 25th reunion Harvard novel joined this group in 1985?

52. Where in Harvard Yard did President James Cheever propose to locate the Decorative Arts Building in **The Memorial Hall Murder**?

53. Nancy Harmon and William Bayer '60 were inspired to write their tacky novel, **Love With a Harvard Accent**, after seeing a movie based on a novel by which Radcliffe graduate?

BUILDINGS & GROUNDS

1. One of the issues of the 1969 student strike was the teaching of ROTC courses on campus. The courses were taught in Shannon Hall. Where is Shannon Hall?

2. Harvard Hall, one of the oldest buildings on campus, originally had a timber roof which soon rotted. That was replaced by a lead roof, and then in turn by its present slate roof. What happened to the lead roof?

3. " 'It is very beautiful—but I think it is very dreadful!' This remark from Verena, called him back to the present. 'It's a real sin to put up such a building, just to glorify a lot of blood-shed. If it wasn't so majestic, I would have pulled it down.' " Can you identify the building in question, and the novel from which this passage comes?

4. Harvard has a Dunster House to commemorate its first president and a Mather House to recall its sixth; why hasn't there been a house named for its third?

Buildings & Grounds

5. Match these illustrious architects with the Harvard buildings they designed:

1.	Joseph Lluis Sert	a)	University Hall
2.	Hugh Stubbins	b)	The Pre-Columbian Art Museum at Dumbarton Oaks
3.	Le Corbusier		
4.	Minoru Yamasaki		
5.	Charles Bulfinch	c)	William James Hall
6.	Philip Johnson	d)	The Science Center
		e)	Pusey Library
		f)	Carpenter Center

6. Where was the John Harvard statue first installed?

7. Where would you be sitting if you could look out the window and see **The Onion**?

8. On the Cambridge end and the downriver side of the Anderson Bridge, there is a tiny plaque which reads: "Drowned in the odour of honeysuckle, 1891-1910." Whom does it commemorate?

9. What Harvard building has a passage from Psalms 8:4 on its northern face?

10. In the 1870s when Memorial Hall was being built, a lot of lumber was left lying about the Yard and undergraduates built bonfires with it. Tutors, proctors, and even President Eliot had to dash out to fight the flames until the president got a brilliant idea which put an end to the bonfires. What was it?

11. What covered Cambridge Common during the years 1917 to 1919?

12. As what was Memorial Hall first used?

13. How long was Memorial Hall employed for this purpose?

Buildings & Grounds

14. What happened to the hundred-year-old elms planted in the Yard during Kirkland's administration?

15. When Massachusetts Hall was erected in 1718-1720, the Massachusetts General Court was pleasantly surprised by what eventuality?

16. Which one of the following is **not** a use to which Holden Chapel was put during its lifetime?
    a) Lumber room
    b) Fire engine house
    c) Dissecting room
    d) Dining hall
    e) Chemistry lecture room
    f) Army barracks

17. About 1720, what small structure was located just south of Massachusetts Hall?

18. For at least how many years did the college engage in the activity which took place in this building?

19. What was known as the "University Minor"?

20. What other structure located near University Hall in the early 19th century was cause for auditory disturbances?

21. Where was the famous "Liberty Tree," or "Rebellion Elm," located?

22. Where were Harvard commencements held between the two World Wars?

23. What is now the second oldest Harvard building still standing? (Careful: It does not contain either student quarters or lecture rooms.)

Buildings & Grounds

24. What were the first two buildings in the Yard to house chemistry labs for students?

25. If you can see representations of Columbus, Chaucer, Dante, Leonidas, Dr. Joseph Warren, Leonardo, LaSalle and Marquette, Pericles, and Shakespeare about you, in what three activities might you be involved?

26. Which Harvard president went around the Yard trimming off awkward-looking sprouts of ivy with his pocket knife?

27. How did Professor Howard Mumford Jones describe Memorial Church?

28. What building in Stratford-on-Avon is kept in trust for Harvard University?

29. What building in Settignano, Italy, a few miles from Florence, is owned by Harvard?

30. The proposed design for a Harvard building featured a giant, flat-topped glass pyramid eighty-five feet high; critics called it "instant Giza," "banal symbolism," and "a cross between Camelot and Disneyland." What was the proposed building and who was its designer?

31. From 1850 to 1855, what ran north from the present site of Austin Hall?

32. The asphalt which curves southwest from Harvard Square through Brattle Square down Eliot Street to where it

Buildings & Grounds

meets John F. Kennedy Street follows the course of what 17th-century Cambridge landmark?

33. Where is the Harvard Forest located?

34. In 1826 the college's first sets of parallel and horizontal bars, trapezes, and flying rings were erected. Where were they located?

35. True or False: The structure on the north side of the Science Center is called Paine Hall.

36. What is notable about the soldiers departing for war in the World War I memorial mural by John Singer Sargent in Widener?

37. Does the John Harvard statue have a moustache?

38. Why are the steps and bricks in front of Hollis and Stoughton dented?

39. When will Harvard's lease on the Arnold Arboretum have to be renewed?

40. What building presently stands on the site of the circular brick structure that was known as the "Old Gym"?

41. When Harvard wanted to tear down Boylston Hall in 1959, how did the university plan to get around the Boylston will that said income from its bequest would go to Harvard only so long as the walls of Boylston Hall remained standing?

Buildings & Grounds

42. How was Widener Library defaced in 1963?

43. What is the tallest Harvard building?

44. When Katherine Ward Lane's rhinoceros statues at the Biology Labs were unveiled in 1930, what items had been added the night before the ceremony?

45. What are the names of those rhinoceri?

46. What Harvard property is located in the District of Columbia?

47. Which Harvard building contains a fifty-foot waterfall and why?

48. Can you name the two prospective sites for the Kennedy Library which preceded its final location at Columbia Point?

49. What Harvard building today stands closest to the location of the Old College of 1638?

50. Many alumni are unfamiliar with even the most visible Harvard landmarks. In the novel **Class Reunion**, for instance, the main gate to the Yard is twice identified erroneously as _____.

51. An even more common error is to call the bridge over the Charles the Larz Anderson Bridge. What is its correct name?

ASSESSMENTS OF THE COLLEGE AND ITS MEN

1. Who said, "I am not aware that **any one single thing** is well taught to the Undergraduates of Harvard College. Certainly I left it without knowing anything."

2. An alumnus of the class of 1858 said to an alumnus of the class of 1886, "So you are trying to teach philosophy at Harvard. I once tried to teach history there, but it can't be done. It isn't really possible to teach anything." Name the two instructors.

3. Commissioned to do a mural for the Holyoke Center penthouse, an abstract painter had this to say about the experience:

    After working in Cambridge for a few days and going to all those horrible Faculty Club lunches I found the air shuttle to New York didn't give me enough time to regain my composure. So I took to going back by train. I'd get on the sleeper with a bottle of Scotch and by the next morning I would just about have recovered from Harvard.

    Who was he?

Assessments

4. What did McGeorge Bundy, dean of the Harvard faculty, have to say about the professors?

5. A character named "Silence Dogood" wrote the following about Harvard students in the Boston **Courant** for May 14, 1722:

   ...they learn little more than how to carry themselves handsomely, and enter a room genteely (which might as well be acquired at a Dancing School), and...they return, after abundance of trouble and Changes, as great Blockheads as ever, only more proud and self-conceited.

   Who was this upstart sixteen-year-old?

6. Who wrote, "Harvard, or any university, is an incredible mirror maze of fake self-perceptions; only a little fool who never questions nor examines can get out without embarassment or injury"?

7. The Harvard Man has that evil pustular monastic look to him, that nasty glazed masturbatory eye. His whole demeanor is an admixture of calculated lymphatic inattention and zeroidal learning. That slow walkathon haberdashery flounce has a caste meanness that in its way surpasses anything I know. But so much for cash-register education in America.

   Who wrote this?

8. Reporting on phone system traffic for the Boston **Transcript** in 1923, a member of the class of 1924 wrote: "Note the abnormality of the 1:30 point when most people are having luncheon in the business sections. Here the telephone seems to be fairly humming

Assessments

with the calls which the Harvard student is making to his dean, his athletic manager, and his bootlegger." Who was this intrepid reporter?

9. Shortly after he was named a professor of philosophy, what 1863 graduate wrote his sister that "although I serve Harvard College to the best of my ability, I have no **affection** at all for the institution, and would gladly desert it for anything that offered better pay"?

10. This Harvard professor, an 1886 alumnus, once said that Harvard was a place where "much generous intellectual sincerity went with such spiritual penury and moral confusion as to offer nothing but a lottery ticket or a chance at the grab-bag for the orphan mind." Who was he?

11 Assessing a typical commencement, who said, "First-time visitors to the scene are rather horrified at what appears to be rank confusion, but then they remember that this is, after all, Harvard where conformity, even for self-preservation, has been elevated to the rank of an original sin"?

12. Everyone is eager to acknowledge her past services. All American citizens are proud of the array of great men whom she has sent forth to serve and grace the country; but, like some other universities, she is falling behind the age. Her glory is declining, even in its external manifestations; and it must decline as long as the choicest youth of the community are no longer sent to study within her walls.

The author of this passage is Harriet Martineau; about what decade in Harvard's history did she make this dismal pronouncement?

13. For generation after generation, Adamses and Brookses and Boylstons and Gorhams had gone to Harvard College, and although none of them, as far as known, had ever done any good there, or thought himself the better for it, custom, social ties, convenience, and, above all, economy, kept each generation in the track. Any other education would have required a serious effort, but no one took Harvard College seriously.

Who wrote this?

14. Which Harvard president complained, "When I was asked to come to this university, I supposed I was to be the head of the largest and most famous institution of learning in America. I have been disappointed. I find myself the submaster of an ill-disciplined **school**."

15. Who first said, "You can always tell a Harvard man, but you can't tell him much"?

16. What were President Edward Holyoke's deathbed words about his job?

17. When Estelle Parsons came to the Loeb Drama Center in the one-woman play **Miss Margarida's Way**, a Harvard undergraduate persisted in tossing paper airplanes on stage. She called him down to the front of "class" and made him eat one of his airplanes, during which act he grinned mischievously at his fellow "classmates." What line did Parsons ad-lib about Harvard students at this point?

Assessments

18. In 1780, President Josiah Langdon was forced to resign partly as a result of a student memorial addressed to him in these words: "As a man of genius and knowledge we respect you; as a man of piety and virtue we venerate you; as a President _____."

19. Complete this old joke from the New Deal days: "The quickest way to Washington is _____."

20. Who wrote in his journal shortly after leaving school in 1900, that "Harvard feeds subjectivity, encourages an all consuming flame + that, in my mind, is an evil in so impersonal a world. Personality must be kept secret before the world"?

21. Who said, "Harvard doesn't teach reality or necessity. If I had a son, I'd send him to West Point"? (Hint: He also calls his company "the West Point of the dance.")

22. Which linguist and U.S. senator from California (**not** an alumnus) once said, "Theoretically, I should be immune to the impact of any label or symbol, but that Harvard label has always bothered me. Something happens to me when I'm in the presence of a Harvard man—I sort of lose my confidence, even though I know some of them are really stupid asses."

23. Cornelius Conway Felton, president of Harvard between 1860 and 1862, once

said, "There is no more comparison between the pleasure of being professor and president in this college than there is between _____ and _____."

HISTORY PART II

1. The college took up a subscription in the 1670s to build Old Harvard Hall. One resident of Medfield, a Thomas Mason, promised one and a half bushels of corn but was scalped in King Philip's War before he could make good. When the Medfield subscription list was published two centuries later, a descendent in the seventh generation, Daniel Gregory Mason, AB 1895, decided to cover his ancestor's debt. How did he make payment?

2. The Rev. Urian Oakes served as president **pro tempore** for four years before accepting the full presidency in 1680. How long did he serve?

3. In October 1681, members of the Old North Church sent a letter to the General Court concerning Harvard which said, "though wee could be glad to help a Sister that has no Breasts, yet wee see not what Rule of Charity or reason, requireth us to cut off our own Breasts, that our Sister may be Supplyed. . . ." What were they talking about?

History II

4. Harvard's fifth president, John Rogers, was installed in August 1683. Late that year he noticed that the next commencement, scheduled for July 2, would coincide with a total solar eclipse, and had the ceremony moved up a day. Commencement was held on July 1. What happened the next day?

5. Until 1700, what was the sole requirement for an AB degree at Harvard?

6. Enraged at being passed over for the college presidency in 1707, and saying he feared "the dear infant should be strangled in the birth," Cotton Mather tried to divert donations intended for Harvard to what other recently-founded college?

7. On January 16, 1764, the General Court of Massachusetts opened session in Harvard Hall. Why was it not at the State House?

8. What happened at Harvard Hall eight days later?

9. Name the one book from John Harvard's library that survives to this day.

10. The General Court of Massachusetts took possession of Harvard College in 1770 by act of sovereign authority and held its sessions in the new Harvard Hall for the next three years. Why?

11. Harvard president Samuel Locke resigned in December 1773 for reasons that were a mystery until the 20th

History II

century when the diary of Yale's president Ezra Stiles, AB 1778, were published. What was the cause of Locke's resignation?

12. Where were Harvard classes held between October 1775 and June 1776?

13. Out of fifty-six signers of the Declaration of Independence, how many were Harvard men?

14. The eminent scientist John Winthrop received Harvard's first honorary LL.D. in 1773. Who received the second?

15. Why were Harvard students dismissed from school between November 1777 and February 1778?

16. Who was treasurer of Harvard College from 1773 to 1777, never reported the accounts to the Corporation, and died in 1793 still owing the college 1,054 pounds?

17. In 1781 the Committee of Overseers under Hancock observed that "there is an institution in the University, with the nature of which the Government is not acquainted, which tends to make a discrimination among the students." What was this sinister organization?

18. Which is older, the U.S. Constitution or the Harvard Medical School?

19. Until the 1820s, the Harvard faculty was known officially as _____.

History II

20. According to Noah Webster, what college was founded by Orthodox Calvinists of the Connecticut Valley "to check the progress of errors which are propagated from Cambridge"?

21. What was the color of the ribbon with which President Josiah Quincy's daughters tied up Harvard diplomas in the 1830s?

22. President Quincy was distressed at having to confer an honorary LL.D. upon the U.S. president, whose visit in 1833 prompted the observation: "Preparations for a public funeral—certainly for his—could not have been made less cheerfully than ours for his welcome." Who was this chief executive?

23. One night in August 1843, students and alumni gathered at the college armed with muskets. What were they expecting?

24. What former Congressman, minister to Great Britain, and Massachusetts governor was offered the Harvard presidency in late 1845, felt it was no "eligible retreat for a man of literary tastes," and allowed himself to be selected "reluctantly, with great misgivings"?

25. When Charles Sumner gave a Free-Soil speech in the Cambridge Lyceum Hall, his friend Longfellow compared the beauty of Sumner's language and the shouts, hisses, and "vulgar interruptions" that met it to _____.

History II

26. In 1848 people protested the possibility that a black student named Beverly Williams would be admitted to Harvard. What was President Everett's reply?

27. The minutes of an 1850 Harvard Medical School faculty meeting noted that Dr. Webster was not in attendance, that his professional associates "respectfully took note of action by the civil authorities," and that they had voted to fill the vacancy that existed "in Dr. Webster's absence." What's the story here?

28. President Everett effaced the name "Harvard" from all official publications during his administration, and insisted the school be known as _____.

29. The Boston courtroom gallery where Professor Webster's trial was held had a capacity of a hundred persons, and the trial lasted eleven days. How many people got to see a part of the trial?

30. The only subject added to the curriculum during the term of President James Walker (1853-1860) was music, which was ironic because _____.

31. For its first century, what did the Harvard Medical School require of its degree candidates?

32. When President Eliot proposed to hire Henry Adams in 1870, the latter protested, "But, Mr. President, I know nothing about Medieval History!" What was Eliot's reply?

43

History II

33. The Harvard Corporation voted to reform the Medical School in 1871, especially after the president of the Board of Overseers, Charles Francis Adams, related what information?

34. At the beginning of President Eliot's term, the Divinity School was humorously described as consisting of "_____."

35. When President Eliot chided Princeton for having only one professor of history, what was President McCosh's testy reply?

36. True or False: Stanford University was founded when Leland Stanford, wanting to make a large bequest, was kept waiting in President Eliot's outer office too long and stormed off to establish his own school.

37. Nowadays, graduates are handed their diplomas in ceremonies at their respective houses before being welcomed to the ranks of educated men and women. How did they receive their diplomas in the 'teens of this century?

38. The Harvard chemistry department, including professor James B. Conant, produced what items for the government during the First World War?

SPORTS

1. Starting as a varsity end his senior year season (1947), this boy scored one touchdown in the first game and broke a leg in practice a few days later. A sympathetic coach sent him in during the final moments of the Yale game so he could get his letter—which neither of his older brothers had won at Harvard. Who was he?

2. In the 1870s, the boathouses did not have floating docks. How did students get into their shells?

3. F.W. Thayer, class of 1878 and captain of the baseball team for three years, invented what article that revolutionized the game?

4. What positions did Thayer play?

5. What did Prof. LeBaron Briggs often say whenever he sat at Soldiers Field with the Unitarian minister Edward Everett Hale?

6. Which Harvard squash player never lost a collegiate match in school and went on

45

Sports

to defeat the twelve-time winner of the North American Open, the Pakistani Sharif Khan, a year out of school?

7. What was distinctive about Harvard football uniforms in the 1922 Yale game?

8. On May 19, 1945, the Radcliffe crew raced the Harvard crew on the Charles. This event, viewed by thousands and covered extensively by the media, ended in what way?

9. Seven Harvard students were arrested in New Haven for creating a disturbance the night of the first Yale game in 1875. What were they fined?

10. Track meets were first held informally in 1874. Who hung up the first Harvard mile and half-mile records?

11. Finish this bit of doggerel entitled "Bedtime Story" and composed by soccer coach John F. Carr '28 in the '30s:
    > On Friday the coach addressed the squad:
    >   "We've got to win tomorrow,
    > And any player who stays out late
    >   Will do so to his sorrow.
    > The game's away, and to get your rest
    >   And be ready to leave at seven,
    > I want you all in bed by ten—
    >   _____!"

12. Which sport generated so little interest when it was introduced at Hemenway Gym at the turn of the century that it was abolished from 1909 to 1920?

13. So he would get his "H" senior year, this 1912 graduate was put in the final in-

46

Sports

ning of the Yale game. He struck out at bat, but tagged the Yale runner out to end the game. He hated his team's captain so much that he immediately dashed off the field with the ball, to which the captain of the winning team is traditionally entitled. Who was this upstart?

14. What **New York Journal** writer reported on an October 31, 1896, football game against the Carlisle Indian School with the words, "It was understood beforehand that the Indians were sure winners. Everybody declared that the Harvard team was composed mainly of cripples, and everybody recited the glory of the aborigines."

15. Prof. Charles R. Lanman, known throughout the world for his work in Sanskrit, tirelessly rowed the Charles through his eighties. How many miles did he estimate he rowed altogether?

16. Wade Welch, who played varsity goalie for Harvard in 1964-65, co-authored a sports book in 1985. Its subject was:
    a) football   d) golf
    b) swimming   e) hockey
    c) squash   f) tennis

17. In 1882 the faculty voted on strict amateur rules for college sports, including a ban on professional trainers. How did the Harvard Base Ball Club sneak around this rule in the winter of 1890-91?

Sports

18. During the 1982 Yale game, what happened on the forty-five yardline with 7:45 remaining in the second quarter?

19. When George Plimpton '48 played quarterback for the Detroit Lions in an exhibition game in 1963, how did he do?

20. What Harvard guard was known to the press as the "Baby Face Assassin"?

21. In the 1933 Holy Cross game, Harvard was inside the ten yardline but the rhythm of its attack was broken when players on both teams got down on hands and knees to _____.

22. Coach Jean Louis Danguy was famous for his instruction, "You hold heem like a bird and not so tight you keel him and not so loose he fly away." To what "heem" was M. Danguy referring?

23. What did goal coach "Skeets" Canterbury do about the fact that 90% of hockey goals scored came from rebounds off the goalie too far out to be cleared?

24. What remark about Harvard captain and All-American Barry Wood in the 1931 Dartmouth game got pioneer CBS sportscaster Ted Husing banned from Harvard Stadium?

25. Harvard students brought home six gold medals for the U.S. from the 1896 Olympics, the first modern Olympic Games. Can you name the events?

Sports

26. In what year did Harvard make its one Rose Bowl appearance?

27. What team did Harvard face in that game and who won?

28. Which Pasadena locals were guests on the Harvard bench?

29. Lindsay Fischer '56 made his mark in the ski jumping world during the 1954-55 season by _____.

30. During World War II, no one was allowed into the Hemenway Gym, where holes were cut in the walls and acid ate the pure maple floors. What was going on in there?

31. How many balls would put a batter on base in 1879?

32. What kind of animal was the Yale mascot in the late 1880s?

33. In 1979, Yale was one of seven unbeaten major football teams in the nation. It ranked first in overall defense (166.4 yards per game), first in rushing (65.4 yards per game), and had the third longest winning streak (behind Alabama and Florida State). CBS-TV ranked it tenth in the nation, tied with Grambling. When Harvard met Yale in New Haven on November 17, with a 2-7 record, what happened?

34. In Yale's 1887 win over Harvard, the Elis' center, Pa Corbin, gained considerable yardage to set up a field goal with what ingenious play?

Sports

35. What was the first intercollegiate athletic event ever held in the United States?

36. Lacrosse captain Nelson Cochrane '32 astonished a Stevens defenseman when he threw up his left forearm to ward off a blow and snapped his opponent's stick in half. How did he do it?

37. On the eve of the 1934 Yale game, who was pictured on the front page of the **Crimson**, and what was he doing?

38. Which future Harvard professor and poet saw quite a bit of action as a Yale substitute in the 1913 Game?

39. Who was captain of the 1899 baseball team and winner of the prize bat for the highest batting average?

40. The Harvard/Yale track team defeated Oxford/Cambridge in the Stadium on July 23, 1921. Edward Gourdin '21 set a world record in the broad jump with 25'3" and barely edged his broad jump rival in the 100 with a 10.2. Who was the sophomore from Caius College twice defeated by Gourdin?

41. How many seasons did Saul Marsch '47 play guard for the Celtics?

42. Chess player Lorin Deland introduced what infamous football tactic in the 1892 Yale game?

43. What future U.S. senator played fullback for Harvard in 1952 and 1953?

Sports

44. When Waseda University made its second visit to the U.S. in 1927, the team had clever fielding but weak hitting. Harvard beat the Japanese by one run, perhaps partly because of what assistance from a Harvard junior varsity ballplayer?

45. According to the **Second H Book of Harvard Athletics**, what sport was once said by the **Encyclopedia Britannica** to be a popular intramural activity at Harvard as early as 1780?

46. True or False: All American defenseman Davey Johnston '63 never scored a single goal in his senior year hockey season.

47. Who scored Harvard's only touchdown in the 21-7 loss to Yale in 1955?

48. Which school with only 254 students upset mighty Harvard on the football field 6-0 in 1921?

49. What was this team's nickname?

50. What distraction during the 1903 Princeton baseball game enabled Harvard to escape a 6-0 shutout and manage a more respectable 6-5 loss?

51. Harvard track had its origins in 1873 as an offshoot of what other sport?

52. True or False: The term "Ivy League" is only one century old.

51

Sports

53. How did Clarence Dillon '05 react when he received a phone call in the middle of the night which informed him the old Soldiers Field Locker Building was being destroyed by fire?

54. The 1949 football team compiled a 1-8 record, including a 29-6 loss to Yale. This prompted **Boston Herald** sportswriter Bill Cunningham to comment that Harvard was "champion of Middlesex county only because _____."

55. What was Richard Clasby's remark when officials nullified his ninety-seven-yard touchdown run in the 1952 Dartmouth game for a minor infraction?

56. How did the Yale crew win the 1870 race but lose the decision to Harvard?

57. How did the 1932 Harvard soccer team acquire Yale's jerseys?

58. John Kirkland Clark introduced basketball at Harvard in 1899-1900 while he was attending Harvard Law. What curious distinction does he hold?

59. At the 1923 Intercollegiate fencing championships held in the Grand Ballroom of New York's Hotel Astor, what embarrassing thing happened to Harvard's Ed Lane?

60. Pop Warner, coach of the Carlisle Indians, fooled a few opponents in 1908 by sewing half-leather, football-shaped pads on the elbows of the jerseys of his halfbacks and ends. Nobody could tell who had the ball. How did Harvard

Sports

coach Percy Haughton handle this problem after a furious Syracuse coach tipped him off before the Harvard-Carlisle game?

61. Harvard's first intercollegiate football opponent was not a New England team. Who was it?

62. In 1914, a so-so Harvard hockey team held Princeton's great Hobey Baker in check during regulation time 1-1. Who scored the winning goal for Harvard after forty minutes of "sudden death" overtime play?

63. On the morning of the 1950 Princeton football game, the **Crimson** declared, "Two powerful elevens will take the field in Princeton's Palmer Stadium this afternoon." What was the punchline that followed?

64. What was Yale's answer to the Harvard band's gigantic bass drum in the 1975 edition of the Game?

65. John Eusden '44, captain of the 1943 swim team, has major swimming letters from which two institutions?

66. In the early 1880s, a field goal was worth how many touchdowns?

67. What interesting base run by Edward Buckley '42 was made while the umpires' eyes were glued to a long, high hit near the foul line?

68. What was the name of the varsity crew coaching launch from 1910 to 1926?

Sports

69. Why did no Harvard varsity football players receive their H's in 1897?

70. What sort of glove did catchers have in the first decade of Harvard baseball?

71. How did Harvard win its 1915 track meet with Yale on the Monday after the meet?

72. Edward McGrath '31 never played with the big leagues, but he found them more rewarding than almost any other Harvard baseball player. How?

73. Tiny Maxwell, the 300-pound referee who stuttered, was used by Eli Malcolm Aldrich as a buffer during the 1921 Yale game. Aldrich dodged around Maxwell from side to side until he could break away for a 30-yard gain. What was the ref's reaction?

74. Which undergraduate golfer never played for Harvard but received an H anyway, and how?

75. Wendell Baker's world-record 440 in 1886 (47.75 seconds) was especially notable for what reason?

76. In the April 16, 1927, game against Bates College, a batter slapped a line drive up the sleeve of pitcher Roy "Spike" Booth '27. How did the umpire call the play?

77. In the first decade of American football, a team could retain possession of the ball if it gained five yards in three rushes or _____.

Sports

78. Between 1901 and 1912, Harvard scored one field goal and not one touchdown against Yale. How close to the Blue goal did the Crimson get in the 1907 Game?

79. In Harvard's first intercollegiate soccer game, played on April Fools' Day, 1905, how did goal tender Alfred Kidder '08 score the winning (and only) goal—for Haverford?

80. When Harvard faced defending Eastern Intercollegiate boxing champion University of Syracuse in 1933-34, what psych-out maneuver did 115-pound Tommy Curtin employ?

81. Which 1974 Ivy League football game took place outside the Stadium a few hours before the Yale game, and probably set a record for most number of players wearing glasses?

82. Which Carlisle player single-handedly defeated a strong Harvard team in 1911 by kicking four field goals (two for forty-three yards) and driving seventy yards for a touchdown?

83. Eugene L.C. Davidson '17, Carl Stearns '26, George Karelitz '24, and Joseph Solano '30 are among a number of New England Intercollegiate champions who never received a varsity letter in their sport. What was it?

84. In the 1-1 tie game with Columbia in 1929, how did Thomas Gilligan '31 "retire" a baseball from the game?

Sports

85. Robert Matson '50, captain of the 1950 golf team, remembers a southern tour during which he played two student golfers destined for greatness on consecutive days. Who were they?

86. A clearly superior Harvard team failed to score in the 1899 Yale game, even though fullback Ellis charged at the Blue goal from the one-yard line. What trick prevented him from scoring?

87. Why did Samuel Felton '48 say he had a Ph.D. in field events?

88. The 1923 baseball team was beaten twice by Princeton, who had a catcher and shortstop named _____.

89. In Yale's 1952 rout of Harvard 41-14 which Yale player scored his team's final point by catching the extra point after the Elis' sixth touchdown?

90. Conscientious Paul Withington '12, captain of the track team, was bothered by the fact that he finished last in the two-mile at the 1912 Yale meet and thus contributed no points in his teammates' sizable defeat—even though he had been painfully ill during the race. How did he make atonement in the IC4A meet in Philadelphia two weeks later?

91. 1903 was the first year the rules allowed a quarterback to run the ball, but only if he crossed the line of scrimmage within five yards from the point where the ball was put into play. How did this change the appearance of Ivy League fields between 1904 and 1910?

Sports

92. How did Dave Morse score the winning run all the way from first base in the 1961 Holy Cross baseball game?

93. In the Crimson's 2-0 soccer defeat of Dartmouth in 1929, who was the opposing team's captain with whom Alexander Stollmeyer '30 shook hands before the game?

94. Wayne Johnson '44 is unique in Ivy football history for what reason?

95. Squash team captain George Black '39 never lost a match to Yale or Princeton, but had coach Jack Barnaby chewing his knuckles at every meet because _____.

96. Where was the first Harvard baseball diamond?

97. Who won the 1968 Harvard/Yale Game?

HARVARD IN FILMS

1. In what 1907 Biograph film do two Harvard students have a spirited fight over a girl?

2. Who played McAndrews, the religion major in the 1926 film **Brown of Harvard**?

3. The screenplay for **Brown of Harvard** was written by Donald Ogden Stewart, a graduate of what college?

4. In the half-time locker scene the Harvard coach yells, "There's 80,000 people out there and half of them love Harvard!" What's wrong with his analysis?

5. What is the Yale cheer recorded by the titles in **Brown of Harvard**?

6. In what 1926 film does Mary Astor appear with Lloyd Hughes, who is "Theodore Wayne," the Harvard man?

7. Who played Benjamin Bradlee '43 in the film **All the President's Men**?

Films

8. In which 1979 Canadian film, originally titled **Spy Games**, does Elliot Gould star as a Harvard instructor who sleeps with students?

9. Who played "Amos Judd," a star polo and crew athlete at Harvard?

10. What cinematic Tarzan also starred in a 1935 film called **Hold 'Em Yale**?

11. Who played Oliver Barrett III in **Love Story**?

12. Identify Oliver's major; identify Jenny's.

13. What number did Oliver wear on his hockey jersey?

14. In which film do Gail Patrick and Carole Lombard pick up a bum to be their butler, who turns out to be a Harvard man?

15. What actor starred as the Harvard-man-turned-bum?

16. In the film **Holiday**, what fact about Cary Grant's character is said to ensure that he will never win Katherine Hepburn?

17. When Professor Nickajak Alvin of the Antideluvian Department measures the cranial index of the hero of **Harvard, Here I Come**, he decides it fits just between the indices of which two hominids?

18. Who is the star of **Harvard, Here I Come**?

Films

19. Who played George Plimpton '48 in the film **Paper Lion**?

20. After four years in Cambridge, this fellow returns to his sleepy hometown in the West, loses control of his snazzy roadster on the muddy main street, and hollers at the local cowpokes, "Out of my way, I'm a Harvard man!" Who played him and what's the movie?

21. In which 1941 film is Errol Flynn admonished with the words, "A Harvard man ought to know how to be gentle"?

22. In **Hold 'Em Yale**, what trick play enables Wilmot to gain yardage in the game against Harvard when he has been told to punt?

23. Which commercial film has the only sequence filmed inside the Indoor Athletic Building?

24. In what film does Robert Young play a Harvard man romanced by Hedy Lamarr?

25. In which 1968 film does Faye Dunaway stroll along the Business School bank of the Charles with Paul Burke?

26. The woman who played Prof. Kingsfield's daughter Susan in the film **The Paper Chase** is known for what television role?

27. Which $36 million flop had a fifteen-minute sequence of a Harvard commencement at the start of its original four-hour version?

Films

28. Where was the Harvard commencement sequence filmed?

29. **Love Story** was not the only film in which Ali McGraw played a 'Cliffie. It was not even the first. What was the first?

30. In which film does the hero say he loves Bergman, only to have a woman ridicule him by saying, "I mean I loved it when I was at Radcliffe," but all that Kierkegaard stuff bores her now?

31. What was the first feature film to use the interior of Memorial Hall as a set?

32. According to Junior Potter in **Son of Paleface**, why can't you put a Harvard man in jail?

33. Who plays the still photographer who shoots a picture of Junior Potter just after he gets out of the bath?

34. After he survives a plane crash, the hero of this film shares a hospital room with a retired general who asks his Radcliffe daughter, "Did you get that stuff from Widener?" What's the film?

35. Name the television movie in which Melissa Sue Anderson plays a Harvard freshman who sleeps with the husband of her Expository Writing teacher.

36. Who played the teacher in the film?

37. **The Last Convertible** was filmed primarily on which college campus?

Films

38. A certain movie featured the plot device of a sacrificial ring on the finger of a rock 'n' roll drummer. At one point, a mad scientist readies a weird-looking gadget with the words, "This should work; it's from Harvard." Which film is this?

39. Name two architectural anachronisms that appear in **The Bostonians**.

40. In what film does William Hurt play a researcher affiliated with the Harvard Medical School?

41. Which 1979 film concerned the story of student radicals at Harvard in the late '60s?

42. What actor played Bill King, the Harvard student who scandalizes his classmates by saying, "Suppose we don't beat Yale, what difference does it make? It's only a football game," in **H.M. Pulham Esquire**?

STUDENT LIFE

1. Were Harvard students ever taught that the sun revolves around the earth?

2. His more recent counterparts have been called "grinds," "wonks," or "nerds"; in the mid-19th century, this type of student was known as a _____.

3. Students at Harvard today complain of overcrowding if they have to share a bedroom, but in the Old College in the 17th century, students often had to share a _____.

4. The entire sophomore class was dismissed from school for the year on May 29, 1834. What had they done?

5. Seventeenth-century morning bever, or breakfast, consisted of two items for which the Harvard student was charged about a halfpenny. What were they?

6. When the college bible was stolen from chapel and sent by express to the Yale librarian around 1850, what group

Student Life

claimed responsibility by writing its name on the flyleaf?

7. Eighteenth-century students indulged in a little dodge they called "hogueing." What was it?

8. In the late 1960s, the master of Adams House was said to have seen a boy and a girl coming out of the boy's room one morning, a clear violation of parietal rules. How did this administrator deftly handle the situation?

9. For how many years in Harvard's history did all students have to endure an annual oral examination?

10. How many subjects a day did a student face in the 17th century?

11. President Thomas Hill earned an undignified nickname when he warned freshmen against overdoing physical exercise, casually mentioning that in weeding his garden he had strained _____.

12. Where did Artemus Ward say Harvard College was located in the 1860s?

13. On April 26-27, 1961, students rioted. Shouting "Latin si, Pusey no!" they stopped cars in the Square, threw raw eggs, and had to be dispersed by deans, proctors, and police with the help of tear gas. What were they protesting?

14. Aside from Greek and Latin, what other language was a compulsory subject at Harvard for its first 119 years?

Student Life

15. Which three eminent Harvard alumni (who were not members of the faculty) might an undergraduate have seen speaking in Harvard Hall during the years 1770 and 1773?

16. When a Harvard student was too high spirited and tended to disrupt his classmates' studies, he was often punished (from the 18th century right into the 20th) with exile to a country parsonage to be tutored by a Harvard-educated minister. This practice was called _____.

17. In the 17th century, what terrible punishment followed private admonition, public admonition, and public confession, but preceded expulsion?

18. In the 19th century, at what time did the oral entrance examination begin, and how long did it last?

19. What was the name of the society devoted to pranks and mischief which was established in Hollis 13 in 1818, was suppressed in 1834, but survived in secret for about eighty years?

20. When this secret society sent out bogus diplomas in Latin to various important people, which recipient mistook his for an honorary Harvard degree and gratefully donated a surgical library and a collection of surgical instruments to the society in return?

21. If a 17th century student didn't like beer for breakfast, his only alternative was _____.

Student Life

22. In the first few decades of Harvard's history, a campus population of about fifty-five students and instructors drank an average of how many barrels of beer per year?

23. Here is a list of official titles for some Harvard courses offered in the 1970s and their principal or founding instructors. Can you come up with their popular student nicknames?
   a) Social Sciences 11: Tradition and Transformation in East Asian Civilization (John King Fairbank and Edwin O. Reischauer)
   b) History 1360: The Great Age of Discovery, 1400-1530 (John H. "Commodore" Parry)
   c) Visual and Environmental Studies 107: Studies of the Built North American Environment from 1580 to the Present (John B. Jackson)
   d) Natural Sciences 150: The Biology of Cancer (William A. Haseltine)
   e) Anthropology 183 and 184: Human Geography and Geography of the Tropics (Frank Trout)
   f) Fine Arts 13: Introduction to the History of Art (a range of professors)
   g) Psychology and Social Relations 1240: Abnormal Psychology (Brendan Maher)
   h) Social Sciences 162: Moral Dilemmas in a Repressive Society—Nazi Germany (Richard Hunt)

24. For the first fifty years of Harvard's existence, a student could be fined if he were caught using what language in the Yard?

Student Life

25. When a certain lecturer came to speak at Boston Music Hall on January 31, 1882, sixty Harvard students sat up front wearing blond and black wigs, wide ties, knee breeches, and black stockings. Each carried a lily or a sunflower in his hand. Who were they coming to see?

26. > The "black flag of rebellion" was hung from the roof of Holworthy. Furniture and glass in the recitation rooms of University [Hall] were smashed, and the fragments hurled out of the windows. The juniors... voted to wear crape on their arms, issued a handbill with an acute dissection of the President's character, and hanged his effigy to the Rebellion Tree. A terrific explosion took place in the chapel....

    When did this rebellion take place, and what were the students protesting?

27. President Oakes died just before commencement in 1681, and to ensure a sober ceremony, the authorities limited students' wine intake to what amount?

28. Before 1900 Harvard could assume entering students had studied four years of Greek, six years of Latin, and twelve years of math. By 1960, however, as Prof. Howard Mumford Jones observed, "We can be sure that they will have only two things in common. They will have read _____ and _____."

29. What happened on "Bloody Monday," an annual event in the 1840s and 1850s?

30. Students rioted in the triangle between Wadsworth House and Lehman Hall in 1825 over what issue?

Student Life

31. By the 1720s commencements had grown so riotous that the General Court passed a law to fine students twenty shillings for the possession of what substance?

THE WOMEN

1. Which member of the class of 1904 published her autobiography in the **Ladies Home Journal** during her sophomore and junior years for a fee of 3,000 dollars?

2. After whom was Radcliffe College named?

3. "Degrees to women direct from Harvard," stated a **Crimson** editorial in 1894, were only a "question...of time." How many years later did this actually occur?

4. What was known to Radcliffe students in the 1950s as the "Charred Body Book"?

5. Radcliffe College was initially known by the official title of _____.

6. What was its nickname?

7. For the first formal commencement at Radcliffe in 1894, the seniors wanted to wear caps and gowns, but President Elizabeth Cary Agassiz personally requested that they not. Why?

8. Which of the following was **not** the name of a short-lived Radcliffe student publication?
   a) **Radditudes**
   b) **The Better Half**
   c) **Pro tem**
   d) **Halfway Down**
   e) **Percussion**
   f) **Etc.**
   g) **Signature**

9. When did men and women first sit in classes together?

10. For the final exam in one of William James's courses, this 1898 graduate wrote in her test booklet, "Dear Prof. James: I am so sorry but I really do not feel like an examination paper in philosophy today," and walked out into the fresh spring morning. Who was she?

11. Which Harvard English professor taught many courses at Radcliffe, but refused to teach Argument, saying, "We can't obliterate a natural tendency, but why cultivate it?"

12. In 1963, which Harvard professor spoke out against parietal rules with the following words?

    > Once when Harvard College was in part a privileged academy for the socially visible, it needed to assure parents that their more retarded offspring would have the supervision of men of the scoutmaster type who, however ineffectually, would try to protect them from the natural penalties of indolence, alcohol or lust. Otherwise needed and prestigious clients would be committed

to other institutions. All this, happily, is now over. Thousands of men and women clamor for admission for the serious purposes of the University. It can be our part of the bargain that they look after themselves.

13. In 1919, Dr. Alice Hamilton (MD University of Michigan '93) became the first woman to be given a teaching appointment at the Harvard Medical School—under three conditions. What were they?

14. What did Harvard President Conant have to say about coeducation in 1952?

15. In 1905 Radcliffe Dean Agnes Irwin happened to ask a Harvard man if he had ever visited Radcliffe, and was taken aback when he replied, "No, but my pants have." What was the explanation?

16. Dr. Edward H. Clarke, professor at the Harvard Medical School from 1855 to 1872, became a center of controversy—for what reason?

17. Which Radcliffe graduate filmed **It's My Turn**, starring Jill Clayburgh, Charles Grodin, and Michael Douglas?

18. What administrative practice at Radcliffe in the early part of the 20th century, ostensibly put into use to check the health of its freshmen, was cause for some nervousness whenever Harvard men threatened to raid the files?

19. Finish this lyric:
    "Oh, Caesar was a Roman,
    He overpowered Gaul,
    He had the German chieftains
    Obeying beck and call.
    But though he was well guarded
    His end was sad, we see,
    Because he . . . ."

20. In the '40s and '50s, mixers in Radcliffe dormitories were known as _____.

21. What Pulitzer Prize-winning poet co-authored two children's books with Anne Sexton, **Eggs of Things** and **More Eggs of Things**?

22. In the 1940s, why was any Radcliffe student who lived within an hour of campus required to commute?

23. Who gave the name "Lost Generation" to the youth of the '20s?

24. Who grew up with Lizzie Borden in Fall River and eventually won the 1967 Edgar Allan Poe award for best fact crime book from the Mystery Writers of America for **A Private Disgrace**, her book on the Borden murders?

25. What did Al Capp say about 'Cliffies?

26. The eminent economist Joseph Schumpeter gave A's to all female students. What was his reasoning?

27. Why did Harvard refuse Nobel Prize winner Madame Curie an honorary degree?

28. Which novelist wrote a Radcliffe thesis on Yevgeny Zamyatin's **We** and Orwell's **1984** and now lives in Ireland?

29. What play was performed at Radcliffe in 1913 only after extensive cutting because President Briggs thought it "unwholesome" and its author a "dangerous" and "poisonous" person?

30. Ture or False: The older Quad houses have hooks on the doors and walls because doors had to be propped open during gentlemen's visits to maintain propriety.

31. Which '62 graduate majored in Middle Eastern history under Sir Hamilton Gibb and wrote her thesis on King Faisal's government in 1920 Syria?

32. Constance Mary Katharine Applebee, a graduate of the British College of Physical Education, came to the United States in 1901 to take a Harvard Summer Course in anthropometry, the study of comparative human body measurements. On a hot August day, at a concrete slab near the Harvard gymnasium, she gave the first demonstration of _____ anyone had ever seen in the United States.

33. In an assessment of Radcliffe College in 1909, who posed the question, "Has Radcliffe College been a vampire sucking the life-blood of the University?"

34. According to Jules Feiffer, how do you impress a 'Cliffie?

35. When asked why she didn't consistently adopt the female viewpoint in her work, which '51 graduate replied, "I want to distance myself from my books. That's one of the reasons I write science fiction. I like to write about aliens. Men are aliens, too. I like the alien point of view"?

36. This Radcliffe graduate was wearing a halter top at her agent's office in the late '50s when a struggling young actor happened by and bit her stomach. He later called up to ask her if he could do it again. Who was the bitten and who was the biter?

37. Which Radcliffe graduate's first film role had her acting opposite Jack Nicholson and Warren Beatty?

38. What 1980 Pulitzer Prize winner's column appears in over 250 newspapers?

39. Which 1933 graduate said, "I never took a Ph.D. It's what saved me, I think. If I had taken a doctoral degree, it would have stifled any writing capacity."

40. Trained and prepared for an operatic singing career, but thwarted by a serious thyroid condition, which 1925 alumnus became a full-time book critic for the **Nation** and was nominated for the Pulitzer in 1982 for her own book, **Mrs. Harris: The Death of the Scarsdale Diet Doctor**?

41. About which Radcliffe graduate's 1985 novel did John Fowles say, "[It] earns

the same shelf as Henry James and Edith Wharton"?

SCHOOL DAYS:
THE ANTICS OF FAMOUS PEOPLE WHEN THEY WERE STUDENTS

1. In his junior year, the future historian William Hickling Prescott sustained an injury to his eye which resulted in much suffering and ultimate blindness. What happened?

2. This member of the class of 1889, the future chairman of U.S. Steel, was appointed by the Delphic Club to find a way for the club to evade the state liquor law which forbade clubs to keep bars. His reaction to his appointment: "It seems rather queer to me because I don't drink, however, I... believe in the inalienable right of every man to make a beast of his self whenever he wishes to." The name of this libertarian?

3. Why was John Reed rusticated?

4. Which member of the class of 1938 came to school as an "adolescent socialist and Zionist," helped organize a boycott of German goods in Boston and was driven off by the cops for picketing Woolworth's, but ended up studying Chinese?

79

5. Having mastered Hebrew, Latin, Greek, and German (and having worked on Arabic in his teens so he could read the Koran), this 1887 graduate tackled Sanskrit in his second year at Harvard. What is his name?

6. The night he was initiated into the Porcellian Club, this member of the class of 1880 got so drunk on wine that the ensuing hangover caused him to drink sparingly, if at all, for the rest of his life. Who was he?

7. What member of the class of 1904 said, "I took economics in college for four years and everything I was taught was wrong"?

8. This future ambassador to Great Britain, class of 1912, bought a bus with a friend sophomore year and set up a sightseeing business based at South Station which cleared $5,000 over the next three years. What is his name? (Bonus: What was his first bus called?)

9. This member of the class of 1830 defied a college statute which said students must wear waistcoats of either "black-mixed" or white by wearing a buff vest in his junior year. After several warnings and debates with this student, the Parietal Board of professors and proctors voted "that hereafter, _____'s vest be considered by this Board white." Who was the student?

10. Dean of the Faculty LeBaron Russell Briggs gave this student, a future poet

School Days

and 1915 alumnus, a grade of "yxwzy" for his twenty-seven-page paper "The New Art" in English 5, Advanced Composition. A portion of the paper was read at the 1915 commencement. What was its author's name?

11. What Pulitzer Prize-winning novelist, class of 1932, wandered the streets of Cambridge, rummaging in trash bins for discarded letters, postcards, valentines, cigarette packages, and other interesting found objects?

12. Which member of the class of 1821 was selected class poet only after six other boys had declined the honor?

13. What future U.S. Supreme Court justice was fined ten dollars for breaking the windows of a freshman's quarters in 1861, the year of his graduation?

14. Norman Mailer's first-choice college accepted him, but he came to Harvard instead. What was his first choice and why did he not attend?

15. What was Mailer's undergraduate major at Harvard?

16. This student started at Princeton partly to avoid the shadow of his older brother, but was kept out by an attack of jaundice and eventually entered Harvard in 1936. Who is he?

17. Who received an annual income of $8,000 from his father's inheritance in the late 1870s, when the salary of Harvard's president was only $5,000?

School Days

18. In his sophomore year, what member of the class of 1754 joined with some friends in getting a black servant so drunk at a local tavern that they "endangered his Life," and was degraded four places in class standing "for very much promoting the... Affair"?

19. Before entering Harvard as a junior at age seventeen, this boy attended schools in Paris and Amsterdam, and lived in St. Petersburg for fifteen months, mostly because his father (class of 1755) was a diplomat. Who was this student?

20. Who was the famed librettist, class of 1940, who as an undergraduate boxer took a left hook to the side of his head which caused him to lose the retina and eventually the sight in his left eye?

21. When **Harvard Crimson** editors stole the **Lampoon's** Sacred Ibis in 1953 and presented it to the Russian Delegation Headquarters at the U.N. as a gift to the Soviet Union, the men at the **Lampoon** were not amused. "The Crimson pranksters seem to have forgotten the rights of property," thundered the president of the **Lampoon**. "It's deplorable that they've carried college jokes into the arena of international relations." Who was the outraged president?

22. This future U.S. Attorney General, class of 1948, accumulated a string of C's broken only by D's in Anglo-American Law and the Principles of Economics. Who is he?

School Days

23. This member of the class of 1924 finished his school work in three years and worked as a cub reporter for the old Boston **Transcript** his fourth year while living in Holworthy. Among other things, he attended and reported on secret meetings of the Klu Klux Klan and did a first-night review of Pavlova. Who was he?

24. "Nervous exhaustion" led this naturalist and historian to leave college in the fall of his senior year for a tour of Europe; he returned briefly in the summer of 1844 to pick up his degree. What is his name?

25. What ex-GI and twenty-three-year-old freshman brought to school a cocker spaniel named Smoky, whom he had picked up in Paris?

26. A music major, this member of the class of 1882 published an escapist fantasy called "The New Swiss Family Robinson" in seven issues of the **Lampoon** which later became his first book and earned a letter of commendation from Mark Twain. Name the author.

27. At one point during his freshman year, Conrad Aiken was walking past the Lampoon building when an upperclassman he had never met came reeling out—drunk—and threw his arms around him. "And that," observed a friend, "if Tom remembers it tomorrow, will cause him to suffer agonies of shyness." Who was the inebriated fellow?

School Days

28. Originally a member of the class of 1834, this boy contracted measles at the start of his junior year and left college because of weak eyes. He joined the senior class at Harvard in December 1836, and sold an account of his adventures while away from school for $250 in 1840. It was an instant bestseller. Name the author and his book.

29. Much to the distress of his successors, a certain member of the class of 1800 started the custom of keeping the Hasty Pudding records in rhyme. Who was he?

30. Thrown out of St. Marks School in Southboro for playing with dynamite and then Berkshire School in Sheffield for rum-running from Boston, this future journalist dropped out of the Yale class of 1925, was expelled from the Yale class of 1926, and finally got his degree from Harvard in mid 1929. Who was he?

31. Which Boston Latin graduate knew ancient Hebrew as well as Latin before he scored well enough on College Board exams to receive "high honors" and acceptance to Harvard, but had to peddle newspapers for two years until he was given a pair of scholarships which together met the $400 tuition and could enter in the fall of 1934?

32. This native of Great Barrington, Massachusetts, had to receive his first bachelor's degree from Fisk University before he could enter Harvard as a junior and earn an AB in philosophy in

School Days

1890. He gave a commencement speech on Jefferson Davis. What was his name?

33. "I never wrote for the **Lampoon**; even the text for my sketches was usually supplied for me by the others, who knew the idioms required. My English was too literary, too ladylike, too correct for such a purpose; and I never acquired, or liked, the American art of perpetual joking." Who said this?

34. In his senior year, this fellow was so afraid that the ravishing honey-blonde he intended to marry, Alice Lee, would be taken by somebody else that he sent abroad for a set of French dueling pistols. Who was he?

35. His freshman year, this future U.S. senator had a friend take his Spanish final for him. Both boys were expelled, but this fellow returned to graduate in 1956. What is his name?

36. His undergraduate thesis—"The Meaning of History: Reflections on Spengler, Toynbee, and Kant"—ran to more than 350 pages, after which the government department set a limit of 150 pages for undergraduate theses. Who was the author?

37. Which member of the class of 1908 spent time on academic probation yet received a Phi Beta Kappa key, and how did it happen?

School Days

38. Which 1853 graduate turned down an invitation to join the Porcellian "because he considered that there was too much dissipation among its members," according to his biographer?

39. What native Lithuanian attended Boston University for one year before entering Harvard as a probationary freshman in 1884?

40. When he entered Harvard in 1904 he intended to be a mathematician, but he had some negative experiences with calculus. He turned to history and found the papers for his 1912 doctoral dissertation—the papers of his great-great-grandfather Harrison Gray Otis—in the wine cellar of his grandfather's house. Who is he?

41. Which student founded **Hound and Horn** magazine in 1927 with fellow Gore Hall resident Varian Fry, took it to New York after graduation in 1930, and then let it fold when a greater project offered itself?

42. What 1976 graduate performed with his sister (AB 1973) and a 1939 graduate in a 1962 concert to raise funds for what would become the Kennedy Center?

43. Which avant-garde theater director said of his days at Harvard, "My biggest failure was performing Macbeth, which Archibald MacLeish called the funniest evening he had spent in the American theater"?

School Days

44. Which seventeen-year-old senior made a calotype (an early photograph made of writing paper dipped in solutions of table salt and silver nitrate) of Harvard Hall taken from the window of his room in Massachusetts Hall in 1839?

45. His family disapproved of his desire to be an artist, so they sent him to Harvard. Shortly after graduation in 1800 he wrote his mother: "It is so long since I have mentioned anything about my painting that I suppose you have concluded I had given it up. I assure you I am determined to become the first painter, at least from America." Who was he?

46. Who, after being chosen Class Poet, resigned from Harvard in the spring of 1911 and fled to Europe to begin "his own education," which led to "Irene," a prostitute in London, and T.S. Eliot in Paris?

47. This Yale dropout made Harvard his beat while working for the Boston **Telegram**. He exposed clandestine sex in the Yard, which the dean had tried to cover up, and reported on a dissident instructor who had showed up at faculty meetings wrapped in a Nazi flag and giving the Nazi salute. This reporter finally got admitted to the Harvard class of 1927 after promising Dean Pennypacker that he would sever all ties with the newspaper. Who is he?

48. "What I most retained of my one year with the ROTC was this knowledge of

School Days

how to mount, speed, or slow a horse —which, when I was riding with communist guerrilla units behind Japanese lines in China two years later, proved to be the most valuable skill I learned at Harvard." Who said this?

49. Raised a Jew, what second-year student was baptized an Episcopalian in Trinity Church, Copley Square, on November 22, 1885, by Phillips Brooks?

50. This 1959 graduate wrote a play for a contest at Harvard, won the first prize of $250, and saw his play go on to Broadway. Name the play and its author.

51. The WHRB Orgies are a tradition which started when Harold F. Van Ummersen '43, jubilant over a scholastic achievement, played what series of compositions on the air non-stop?

52. "I played the leading lady in the Institute Theatricals of 1884, and two years later, though I no longer looked at all deceptive in feminine clothes, I was one of the ballet in the Hasty Pudding play." Who said this?

53. At the end of the 1925-26 year, Lucius Beebe conducted a postcard poll of readers of the **Crimson** in which he asked them to vote on the following proposition: "Harvard will be willing to trade President Lowell, President Emeritus Eliot and three heads of departments for a good running backfield and no questions asked." How did the motion fare?

School Days

54. One classmate said of him, "Everyone liked Tom but except for his extraordinary brain power he seemed rather ordinary." Who was he?

55. What student spent his junior year studying art history in Florence, and had a sort of epiphany in August 1929 when he accidentally stumbled on the funeral procession of Serge Diaghilev in Venice?

56. King Philip's War (1675-76) saw battles in Medfield, Groton, and Rehoboth. When the Indian leader King Philip was defeated, he was shot and quartered— Boston receiving his hands and Plymouth his head. Which Harvard undergraduate recalled detaching Philip's jaw from the skull?

57. "I began to write fiction on the assumption that the true enemies of the novel were plot, character, setting, and theme," says this 1949 alumnus, whose first novel, **The Cannibal**, was composed at Harvard and was based partly on his experiences as an ambulance driver in Italy and Germany in World War II. Who is he?

58. Which 1947 graduate lost his virginity in the back of a Model A parked in a lot near Harvard Square?

59. Which Harvard graduate first attended the Junior College of Kansas City and received his AA in 1919 before coming to Cambridge to join the class of 1922 and running off to Paris to study with Nadia Boulanger?

60. In his junior year this fellow wrote and staged **Across the River and Into the Jungle**, in which Kid Congo leads an expedition in search of a movie star whose plane has crashed en route to Johannesburg. The natives are polka-dotted and the cast's writer figure labors over the first sentence of a piece to be published in **Esquire**. Name the playwright.

61. Today this WHRB alumnus covers the White House for NBC-TV, but in the early spring of his senior year at Harvard he was broadcasting live from University Hall on the night of the bust. Who is he?

62. This 1918 graduate, a future author of Pulitzer Prize-winning plays and an Oscar-winning screenplay, enlisted in the Canadian Black Watch in the middle of his junior year, went to France, was gassed twice, and received wounds in both legs at Amiens. What is his name?

63. J. Arthur Greenwood sent a telegram to his parents to report his election to Phi Beta Kappa, but his father threw it in the trash without comprehending it because _____.

64. Which student matriculated in 1651 at age twelve, left school after six months because his parents decided he had a "weak natural constitution of Body," and was tutored for several years by the Rev. John Norton of Ipswich until he joined the senior class of 1656?

65. Which native of Stamford, Connecticut lived in Juneau, Alaska, from ages ten to fifteen, entered Harvard in the sum-

School Days

mer of 1943, and joined the army after failing two courses his first semester?

66. College librarian Thaddeus William Harris said that if Thoreau hadn't been spoiled by Emerson, he would have made a wonderful _____.

67. Who was the youngest student ever to matriculate at Harvard?

68. This boy left school his sophomore year to serve with other young writers in an American ambulance unit in 1917, but soon found himself driving munitions trucks for the French military transport. He finished up at Harvard in 1920 and eventually became a respected essayist and critic. Who is he?

69. This member of the class of 1926 had planned to enter in the fall of 1921, but on a summer trip to Europe he came down with a heavy case of trench dysentery after exploring old mines in Bohemia. Kept out a year by illness, he nevertheless earned his AB in chemistry summa cum laude in three years. Name him.

70. This Somerville native's first published short story, "Proof," appeared in **Astounding Science-Fiction** in June 1942 while he was a junior at Harvard. What is his name?

71. A philosophy and Greek major asked Alfred North Whitehead about his grade. "You've given me a B, and I know I don't know anything," he said.

School Days

Whitehead replied, "Oh, I always give an A to those who are acceptable and a B to those who are no good." Who was the no-good student?

72. What future professor of history and sociology roomed with John Updike in college?

73. A young Ohio bandleader named Guy Lombardo heard a recording of Harvard's Gold Coast Orchestra and was so impressed by the arrangements that he gave the Harvard junior responsible for them a summer job at $125 an arrangement. Who was the boy?

74. What future journalist failed three times to get on the staff of the **Crimson**?

DROPOUTS & SPECIAL STUDENTS

1. His father, uncle, and older brother attended Harvard, and he entered in the same class as John Kennedy. His sophomore year he dropped Banjo Club to join the Young Communist League, writing in his journal, "As an individual, what do I count for? In the YCL I have the Comintern behind me." He left school in his junior year. Who is he?

2. This son of four generations of Harvard alumni dropped out twice. The first time he cut midterms to take out a dancer named Marilyn Miller and the whole chorus of her show, **Passing Show of 1912**, to dinner. Readmitted, he received honors in biology, mathematics, and physics, but left school a second time because memorization bored him. What is his name?

3. His freshman year, this boy acquired a pet alligator named Champagne Charlie, whom he kept frequently drunk on wine. Charlie eventually succumbed to alcoholism and was stuffed and hung

Dropouts & Special Students

up in his owner's room. Who was his owner?

4. What poet left school in 1900 without taking a degree, although he had completed sixteen-and-a-half courses in three years?

5. His company developed an oil drill bit which made him and his son multimillionaires. He dropped out of Harvard in 1894 after one year of study. What was his name?

6. How did Robert Frost catch the chills that threatened to become tuberculosis and were partly responsible for his leaving Harvard in 1899?

7. A special student at Harvard from 1891 to 1893, this young man left school due to ill health and his family's penury (his father had died just before his second year in school)—and became a poet! What was the name of this practical fellow?

8. After one year at Princeton marked by poor scholastic standing and an incident of drunken vandalism, a gold prospecting expedition in the Spanish Honduras, service as a sailor on a Norwegian ship to Buenos Aires, a suicide attempt, a marriage and a son, this twenty-six-year-old came to Cambridge as a special student with the goal of becoming "an artist or nothing." Identify him.

9. He attended Harvard in 1926-27 and from 1929 to 1932, but did not finish. Today he personally holds more than

Dropouts & Special Students

500 U.S. patents, from filters for automobile headlights to World War II anti-aircraft goggles. "I am addicted to at least one good experiment a day," he once said. Who is he?

10. Entering in the same class as Talking Heads' member Jerry Harrison, this coed began singing at the Second Fret after her freshman year and left school a year later. Three years later she was headlining at Max's Kansas City in New York. Who is she?

11. Because he attended for only the 1920-21 school year, this fellow called himself a "quarter-bred Harvard alumnus." As he put it, he "had to drop out to earn a living," and in a few years, while working at Doubleday, he discovered "my field—the minor idiocies of humanity." What was his name?

12. This Florida native formed the nation's first country-rock band, the International Submarine Band with an album called **Safe At Home**, during the year he was at Harvard (1965-66). What was the founder's name?

13. Why was William Randolph Hearst rusticated?

14. William Laurence wrote the following about himself and a classmate in Prof. George Pierce Baker's course in 1914:
> When we were drunk enough, we would go to the Boston Common and stand under a huge elm and lecture passers-by,

Dropouts & Special Students

who, at that hour, usually consisted of sailors and their girls. We'd argue for universal sterilization, as the best solution for the human race. We maintained that the advantage of sterilization was freedom to fornicate to our hearts' content and put the abortionists out of business. We were loud, but our audiences seemed amused, and we always somehow managed to escape arrest.

Who was Mr. Laurence's fellow Cicero?

15. What member of the class of 1901 and future poet had the peculiar hobby of going to Boston pawn shops to see what they would offer him for his watch? (Bad hint: His nickname was "Pete.")

16. Which Harvard dropout was eulogized in song by Emmylou Harris, the Eagles, Poco, and the Rolling Stones?

17. Who came to the U.S. in 1932 on a scholarship to study drama at Yale, spent the 1933-34 year at Harvard, then returned to Europe to become a radio journalist who reported to Americans on the abdication of Edward VIII, the Munich Conference, and the Wimbledon tennis matches?

18. For what was William Randolph Hearst expelled?

19. When this boy entered Harvard College, his uncle Edward was the Boylston Professor of Rhetoric and Oratory, his uncle William an Overseer and a minister who led prayers in Holden Chapel,

Dropouts & Special Students

and his father dean of the medical faculty. But the boy left school on December 4th of his freshman year, and though he was to become a newspaper editor, the author of seven volumes of verse, the most prolific contributor to **The Dial**, and the first biographer of Thoreau, his own biographer called him a failure "as a husband, as a writer, perhaps as a man." Who was this hapless fellow?

20. What was the name this person gave to Harvard in a series of semi-autobiographical letters he published in **The Dial**?

21. Isoroku Yamamoto was the architect of the attack on Pearl Harbor. What was his Harvard connection?

22. A certain Harvard dropout died at age twenty-six. Presumably on his prior instructions, a friend named Phil Kaufman (who had once served time on a drugs conviction at Terminal Island with Charles Manson) stole his body from a baggage ramp at Los Angeles Airport and burned it in the Mojave Desert. What man ordered his own desert cremation?

23. Why did James B. Connolly leave Harvard in a rage the spring of his freshman year, never to return?

24. This aspiring poet was rejected by the **Advocate**. The literary board had him come by to tack a carpet and then told him not to come around anymore. He left school in 1937 after two years' attendance. Who was he?

PHOTOGRAPHS

1. Who is this supposed to be?

2. What is the famous nickname of this statue?

3. Who is this really?

4. This is said to be the fourth most photographed statue in the U.S. Can you name the first three?

99

Photos

5. What is the purpose of this structure?

6. At the time it was built, this building had the distinction of being the costliest building per square foot ever erected in the Boston area. How much did it cost to build?

Photos

7. What is the name of the building to the right?
8. To what building on the left does the elevated tunnel connect?
9. Which library's entrance is in the left foreground?
10. What is the story behind the construction of the elevated passage?

101

Photos

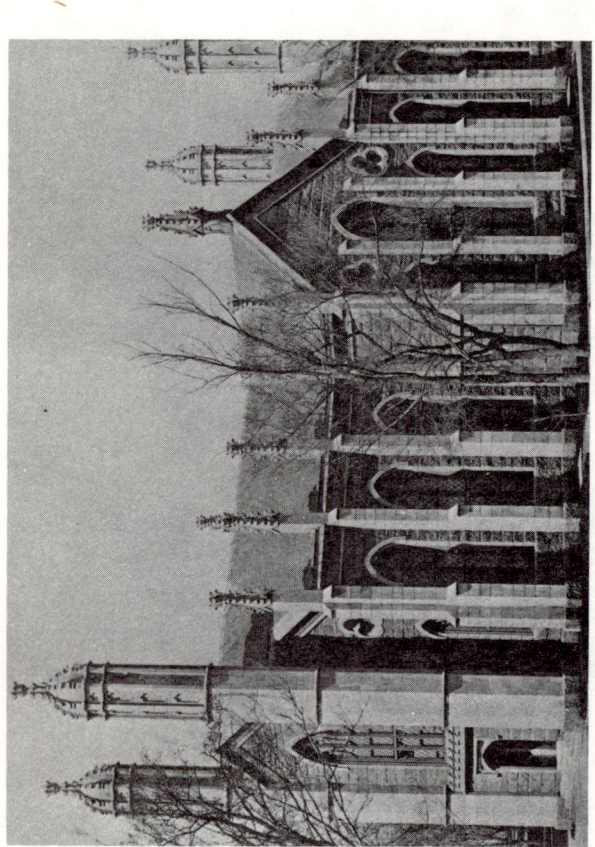

(photo courtesy of the Harvard University Archives)

11. What is the name of this structure?
12. What did it contain?
13. What building now occupies this site?
14. What Harvard building carries this structure's name today?

102

15. What's the name of the building in the foreground?

16. What's the larger building in the background?

17. From what vantage was this photo taken?

Photos

18. What is the name of this structure?
19. What are the four names by which the street in front of this building has been known?
20. What happened to the first owner of this building?
21. To what use is this structure now put?

104

Photos

(photo courtesy of the Harvard University Archives)

22. Built in 1878, razed in 1938, what was this building called?

23. How many years had its donor been out of college when he made a gift of this building?

24. What stands on this site today?

Photos

25. In what town is this corner located?

26. The first house on this street, the one whose chimney sticks up out of the foliage, is #16 and was built in 1812. What famous person lived in it?

Photos

27. This is the entrance to what building?

28. What hall occupied this site until 1982?

29. Do you think this is a lovely entrance?

107

Photos

30. The steeple of which church can be seen here?

31. The roof of what building is visible immediately below the steeple?

32. What building is more prominently visible center left?

33. From what building was this shot taken?

Photos

34. As what is this man popularly known?

35. What name appears on his birth certificate?

36. In what year did he graduate from Harvard College?

37. Where did he execute his doctoral project?

Photos

(photo courtesy of the Harvard University Archives)

38. Built in 1895, this building was known as _____.

39. What other two names did it go by during its lifetime?

40. What structure now occupies this site?

Photos

41. What building is in the left foreground?

42. This is the western end of the structure. When it was first built, at which end did students enter?

43. What building is in the right foreground?

44. What building is in the background?

111

Photos

45. In what town is this mall located?
46. What originally occupied this site and is commemorated by this besmirched monument and playground?

Photos

47. This house dates from 1820. What famous Harvard graduate lived in it between 1822 and 1832?

48. In 1840 a revolving turret was installed in this house so it could become Harvard's first _____.

49. This is not its original location. What building presently inhabits that site?

50. What is the name of this building?

113

51. This is the tower of what Harvard building?

52. What sort of students would you find in this building?

Photos

(photo courtesy of the Harvard University Archives)

53. For what purpose was this building first used?

54. After the original purpose was exhausted, how was this building used?

55. What structure now occupies this site?

115

Photos

56. Who presently lives in the brightly-colored house in the foreground (1985)?

57. What building behind it is mostly obscured by trees?

58. For what is the second building used today?

59. What street lies just beyond the left edge of this photo?

60. What building stands just beyond the bottom edge of this photo?

116

Photos

61. What is the name of this structure?

62. On what street is it located?

63. Where was this building first erected before it was moved here?

64. For what reason were six officers of this building's organization compelled to resign in 1935?

117

Photos

65. What is the first building, with the lions, called?
66. What is the second, with the flag, known as?
67. What is the third building, which reaches closer to the street?
68. What is the name of the street in this photo?

Photos

69. What is the building in the lower right corner?

70. What is the structure with the white pillars beyond it?

71. What is the name of the tiny side street that separates them?

72. Portions of three River Houses are visible in this photo. Can you name them?

Photos

(photo courtesy of the Harvard University Archives)

73. What was the name of this building?

74. What portion of the university did it originally house?

75. Which one of the following did not occupy this building during its history: chem labs, psych labs, The Coop, debate societies, president's office, or bursar's office?

76. Built in 1832, the structure was moved seventy feet south in 1871 to make room for what other building?

77. Which Harvard building occupies this site today?

MISCELLANY

1. True or False: Harvard was the first college founded in the New World.

2. Name the two Harvard instructors whose contracts were not renewed because they used the "mind-expanding" drug psilocybin in experiments on students during the '60s.

3. What name was yelled in the Yard for decades after its holder was graduated in 1900?

4. What objects were dug up in Harvard Yard in 1979 during excavations for the MBTA subway extension and deposited in Houghton Library?

5. What media personality did the **Crimson** push as a U.S. presidential candidate in 1952, leading to a riot in Harvard Square with police violence?

6. Saying, "The place has been named for that Harvard fellow for 300 years, and that's long enough for one person," Cambridge City Councilor Alfred Vellucci

Miscellany

convinced his colleagues to pass a motion to rename Harvard Square for the duration of March 17, 1969. What was the new name?

7. What was the Harvard New College?

8. Soon after a special performance of the Hasty Pudding show "Take a Brace," the U.S. president died. Pudding songwriter Louis Silvers remarked, "It took only one man to kill Lincoln." What president prompted this remark?

9. Finish this lyric: "These are the only ones of which the news has come to Hah-verd...."

10. Which Harvard president was embarrassed by a sister who wrote unconventional poetry and smoked cigars?

11. The 1839 alumnus who wrote **Man Without a Country** had a great uncle who was hung. Name both men.

12. Namesakes were popular in the 19th century. Which one of the following is **not** the name of a recipient of an honorary degree from Harvard?
    a) Alexander Hamilton Vinton
    b) George Washington Hosmer
    c) Thomas Jefferson Sawyer
    d) Paul Revere Frothingham
    e) Quincy Adams Wagstaff
    f) John Milton Fessenden
    g) George Washington Lafayette
    h) Thomas Jefferson Coolidge

Miscellany

13. According to a number of H.P. Lovecraft stories, a copy of what book, the reading of which leads to "terrible consequences," is in Widener Library? Bonus: Who is the author of this evil book?

14. When A. Lawrence Lowell paid a visit to the nation's chief executive, a Harvard functionary was heard to utter what famous line?

15. During final exam period, 1966, The Coop announced an important item would arrive on a Saturday. When samples arrived a day early, The Coop posted a sign that read simply, "IT'S HERE!" and hundreds of impatient students lined up in queues. What were they purchasing?

16. Asa Gray and Alexander Agassiz, professors of botany, acquired an island in Buzzard's Bay for the use of Harvard summer school students. What eventually happened to it?

17. A.K. Ozai-Durani, born to an Afghan nomad tribe and endower of a Harvard lectureship on Indo-Muslim culture, is the inventor of _____.

18. William G. Anderson '39, appointed University Marshal in 1965, sensibly prepared for the job in what way?

19. Harvard's policy is not to confer an honorary degree unless the recipient shows up. Douglas MacArthur, for example, was voted a degree, but never

came in person to collect it. Harvard made an exception in 1945 for what person and for what reason?

20. Future president Thomas Hill went on a collecting trip with Professor Louis Agassiz in 1848, and he explained to the driver of the coach that his passengers were "a set of naturalists from an institution near Boston." How did the driver translate this to another stage driver he met on the road?

21. What is the name of the mythical private school from which preppies issue forth in a steady stream to attend Harvard?

22. Of the following eight men, only one did not receive an honorary degree, but was made up by the author. Which one?
    a) Cotton Tufts
    b) Royall Makepeace Ransom
    c) Heinrich Angst
    d) Rufus Phineas Stebbins
    e) Royal Flint
    f) Moses Sweat
    g) George Frisbie Hoar
    h) Ormsby McKnight Mitchel
    i) Austin Adams Bullock

23. According to Edward A. Weeks, what colorful character is an honorary member of every class and much in evidence at reunions?

24. In the spring of 1942, the **Harvard Advocate** held a party attended by F.O. Matthiessen, Joan Didion, Norman Mailer, and many others in honor of a celebrity who never showed up and

Miscellany

had, in fact, declined an invitation to appear, unbeknownst to nearly everyone. Who was it?

25. Which one of the following could **not** have been seen by Harvard undergraduates on stage at the Club 47 on Mt. Auburn Street in the '60s?
    a) Bonnie Raitt
    b) The Lovin' Spoonful
    c) Jessie Colin Young
    d) Richie Havens
    e) Arlo Guthrie
    f) Canned Heat
    g) Joni Mitchell

26. In 1784, Harvard granted an honorary LL.D. to Marie Jean Paul Roch Yves Gilbert Mochier, better known as _____.

27. How was E.B. White inadvertantly responsible for the switch from Latin to English on Harvard honorary degree citations?

28. George Santayana came to Harvard after studying how many years at Boston Latin?

29. When one undergrad proposed to write a thesis on Arabian music, what did Hancock Professor of Hebrew Crawford H. Toy have to say?

30. The Thomas Cotton Fund was established in 1827 to supplement the miserable income of the President of Harvard. How much is its annual yield today?

Miscellany

31. As an alternative to rationed meats in World War II, the Faculty Club menu began to list what item?

32. Although few ordered this entree, it was kept on the menu long after the war was over as a result of the protests of tradition-minded diners every time it was removed. What was the most recent year it could be seen on the menu?

33. Pick the U.S. president in each group who did not receive an honorary Harvard degree:

    I
    a) Thomas Jefferson
    b) James Monroe
    c) James Madison

    II
    a) Abraham Lincoln
    b) Ulysses S. Grant
    c) Rutherford B. Hayes

    III
    a) William McKinley
    b) Theodore Roosevelt
    c) William Howard Taft

    IV
    a) Herbert Hoover
    b) Harry S. Truman
    c) Dwight D. Eisenhower

34. How did the Delphic Club get its sometime nickname, "The Gas House"?

35. President Nathan Pusey's summer retreat was Hidden House on Mt. Desert Island in Maine. He used to say, "I go there and get out my crowbar." What was he doing?

36. What did professor William James have to say about algebra?

37. Which U.S. president refused the honorary LL.D. voted him by the Governing Boards on the ground that his education was scanty and he didn't know enough to qualify as an eminent lawyer?

Miscellany

38. In the spring of 1922, a seventeen-year-old student at Phillips Exeter Academy who had been admitted to Harvard for the following year died of pneumonia and mastoiditis. His heartbroken father, with an initial endowment of $3 million, founded in his name the _____.

39. A popular witticism that drew upon Charles Eliot Norton's distaste for the cheap and nasty vulgarity of much of American life suggested that his words upon entering Heaven were _____.

40. When a woman college president came to Harvard to find a professor for her English faculty, insisting that he possess a Ph.D., Charles Townsend Copeland supposedly remarked, "Thank God, then we'll not lose _____!"

41. Name the Harvard graduates who either wrote or co-authored the screenplays for the following films: **The Deep, Night of the Hunter, Terminal Man,** and **The Scarlet Pimpernel** (1935).

42. Nathaniel Southgate Shaler, a geology professor in the late 19th century, was appalled by Charles Darwin's lament that a lifetime devoted to scientific research had caused him to lose all interest in the poetry and drama he had enjoyed in his youth. Shaler decided to prove such alienation between art and science was not inevitable by doing what?

43. Which Harvard professor had a lecture hall in the Sorbonne named after him?

Miscellany

44. During the 1983 commencement week, the Harvard Glee Club presented **Ah**, a choral prelude it had commissioned by what composer?

45. Where is one of the world's oldest and largest camellias in an outdoor garden, a specimen of the "John Harvard," located?

46. What other variety of flower has a hybrid presently extant called the "John Harvard"?

47. When the ad agency for McDonald's consulted Professor Larry D. Benson on the proper plural form of "Egg McMuffin," what was his considered opinion?

48. Who suspected his arch-enemy would try to have him killed on the eve of war, wrote to Harvard, Stanford, and Chicago in 1939 to see who was most interested in his papers, and closed the deal with Harvard just before he was assassinated on August 20, 1940?

49. Professor Harry Wolfson's bookcases were so overloaded that he kept books and packets of lecture notes in his ____.

50. What works by T.S. Eliot and e.e. cummings are **not** kept in Harvard's library system?

51. In July 1946, Representative Albert Koorie of New Orleans sponsored in the Louisiana legislature "An act to restore peace, tranquillity and sanity to the United States." Despite what the spon-

Miscellany

sor called nation-wide endorsement of the measure, it passed by a vote of 46 to 12—five votes short of the number needed for enactment—and was tabled. What did the act propose?

52. Which best-selling novelist, with over seventy million copies in sales, has a 1939 Harvard M.B.A.?

53. Which one of the following is not on Stanley Marcus's list of top quality items: Bic Lighters, Sara Lee pound cakes, felt-tip pens, Kleenex, stock options, Levi's jeans, Peugeot pepper mills, or service at Hong Kong's Peninsula Hotel?

54. What was the connection between Harvard and the man known as "Cordwainer Smith"?

55. Thomas Kyd, author of the potboilers **Blood Is a Beggar**, **Blood of Vintage**, **Blood on the Bosom Devine**, and **Cover His Face**, was the nom de plume of what person?

56. In early May of 1976, violinist Lynn Chang '75 played Mendelssohn's **Hebrides Overture** in Forbes Plaza, Holyoke Center, accompanied by what other instruments?

57. During the diploma riots, what was President Pusey's rhyming reply to the students?

58. In 1941 the Fogg Museum's gallery of Romanesque sculpture was host to what incendiary piece of political protest?

Miscellany

59. The November 8, 1947, Harvard Alumni Bulletin reported that **Adventures with a Texas Naturalist** by Roy Bedichek listed a hardy oak indigenous to the sandy plains of southern Texas and eastern New Mexico called **Quercus harvardii**. What is the tree's Harvard connection?

60. In 1936, denizens of the **Lampoon** hoisted a red flag over the U.S. Supreme Court Building. It was fastened so tightly that guards had to do what to remove it?

61. According to Arthur Bloch's **Murphy's Law** and Paul Dickson's **The Official Rules**, what is the Harvard Law?

62. E.J. Kahn's book **Harvard: Through Change and Through Storm** reported that the 25th Reunion liquor bill was $11,000 in 1969. What is it now?

63. On October 22, 1985, in response to student protests, President Bok announced that Harvard would divest itself of stock in any corporation "that teases, intimidates, harasses or otherwise contributes to the demise of _____."

ANSWERS

HISTORY
PART I

1. William Shakespeare

2. books

3. "Newetowne" (which was renamed Cambridge almost six months later)

4. True. Off and on between 1634 and 1638, and certainly on November 17, 1637, Newtown was where the General Court sat.

5. On three hundred acres of land bordering Marblehead, with a good quarter-mile of frontage on the ocean, offered by the city of Salem (Don't ask me why they didn't take it!)

6. Anne Hutchinson, who was soon banished from the Colony

7. a) In England
   b) One
   c) Probably not. Samuel Eliot Morison suggests he made the bequest orally, on his deathbed.
   d) A week to ten days

History I Answers

8. The town of Boston voted to have a grammar school a full year before Harvard was founded, and students attended classes there two years before Harvard was open for business.

9. 329 titles, or over 400 volumes

10. One

11. 279 years. Lionel de Jersey Harvard, a descendent of John's second cousin Robert, graduated with the class of 1915.

12. a) and e)

13. He had flogged students and assaulted his assistant with a walnut-tree cudgel.

14. Students charged she had served mackerel "with their guts in them" and pudding laced with goat's dung.

15. In debtor's prison in England

16. He married a wealthy widow who died two years after they were wed.

17. The Boston/Charlestown ferry

18. 1642

19. Nine

20. Two centuries later, when it was unearthed for the bicentennial and President Quincy had it printed in his history of the college

History I Answers

21. The corpse of "some malefatour" for the purpose of teaching anatomy, but there is no evidence that Harvard ever realized her "quadrennial corpse privilege," says Morison

22. As soon as they heard what the meeting was about, "fifty of them withdrew," and Salem gave nothing.

23. For the first decade, Harvard had a three-year undergraduate course, which President Dunster wanted to extend to four years. So the original class of 1652 was held in school until August 9, 1653, and the original class of 1653 graduated the next day.

24. g)

25. Some students had been fooling with black magic and convinced themselves they had raised the Devil, so the president improvised an exorcism to restore calm.

26. In the form of Indian corn or other produce which they had to convert to legal tender themselves at a loss

27. b) This answer is correct, although it will cease to be in 1990. Harvard did not grant diplomas as a matter of course until 1813, 177 years after its founding. Until then, students who wanted a diploma—usually only those who went abroad—had to pay a fee, often years after graduation.

28. He had voiced doubts about the validity of infant baptism.

History I Answers

29. To expound chapters from the Old and New Testaments to students twice a day

30. Stoughton was the "hanging judge" of the Salem witchcraft trials.

31. He was the only Native American to complete studies at Harvard's "Indian College" in the mid-17th century. He died of tuberculosis within a year.

32. The wife of the grandson who inherited President Chauncy's papers eventually took as her second husband the Northampton community pie-baker, who used those papers to protect the bottoms of his pies from burning. Morison guesses the Harvard president's manuscripts added "a special relish and indigestibility to the standard product of the Connecticut River pie belt."

33. It was the 1200-page Indian Bible, translated into Algonkian and published on the Harvard hand press in 1663.

34. **The Imitation of Christ**, by Thomas á Kempis

35. None

ALUMNI

1. James Otis
2. Horatio Alger
3. Daniel Ellsberg '52
4. William S. Burroughs
5. cartoonist
6. Henry Cabot Lodge, Jr.
7. Erich Segal
8. Cleveland Amory
9. Theodore H. White
10. William Burroughs
11. Tom Lehrer
12. Jerry Harrison of Talking Heads
13. Joni Mitchell
14. John Ashbery

Alumni Answers

15. William Burroughs

16. Leonard Bernstein '39

17. Michael Crichton ("Michael Douglas" he shared with his brother Douglas on a book they co-authored.)

18. John King Fairbank

19. David Halberstam '55

20. Horatio Alger, AB 1852

21. d) He tried to get into the OSS, but deliberately cut off the first joint of one finger and was rejected.

22. Cleveland Amory

23. Michael Crichton '64, MD '69. He was writing his textbook **Five Patients: The Hospital Explained**, which has since been translated into twenty languages.

24. Daniel Ellsberg

25. Michael J. Halberstam '53

26. **The Russians Are Coming, The Russians Are Coming!**

27. He is the only Harvard graduate to be hanged for witchcraft. Judges Samuel Sewall, AB 1671, and William Stoughton, AB 1650, convicted him in 1692.

28. John Trumbull, AB 1773, best known for his four life-size Revolutionary War scenes in the U.S. Capitol rotunda

Alumni Answers

29. Webber had to leave one part undeveloped in the original London production of his musical **Cats** (lyrics by another well-known Harvard alumnus) because he could not find an actor who could sing 19th-century opera and meet the other demands of the show. Hanan could, so for the Broadway production Webber extended the part and composed an aria just for him.

30. Andre Gregory '56 and Wallace Shawn '65, in **My Dinner With Andre**

31. Sir George Downing, who built and named a street for himself in 1682. The street now carries the address of the British prime minister—10 Downing Street.

32. Washington Allston

33. As I was going up the stair,
    I met a man who wasn't there.
    He wasn't there again today.
    I wish, I wish he'd go away.

34. **And the Hippos Were Boiled in Their Tanks**

35. Crichton, six foot nine inches, took the name of a famous dwarf in the English court of Charles I.

36. Frank O'Hara

37. Edward Gorey

38. **The Hunchback of Notre Dame**

Alumni Answers

39. Philip Johnson

40. Virgil Thomson '22

41. Dan Raviv '76

42. George Plimpton '48

43. David Riesman, author of **The Lonely Crowd**

44. Yugoslavia

45. President Truman

46. H.V. Kaltenborn

47. Frank O'Hara '50 was run down by a beach taxi at a vacation resort.

48. Edward Gorey

49. Robert F. Kennedy

50. **Sesame Street**

51. Lincoln Kirstein

52. John P. Marquand '15. His creation was Mr. Moto, the Japanese secret agent.

53. Fred Gwynne '51, also known as Sgt. Muldoon of "Car 54, Where Are You?" and Hermann Munster

54. James R. Schlesinger '50

55. "Casey at the Bat"

56. Philip Johnson '27, whose classmate Lincoln Kirstein stood by him during those days

Alumni Answers

57. Benjamin Bradlee

58. J. Anthony Lukas '55

59. Stanley Marcus

60. Richard Strout '19, **Christian Science Monitor** columnist and **The New Republic**'s "TRB" for over forty years

61. Rutherford B. Hayes

62. "O Little Town of Bethlehem"

63. Tommy Lee Jones

64. Joseph Alsop

65. Art Hoppe '49, columnist for the **San Francisco Chronicle**

66. In the "Saturday Night Massacre," Elliot Richardson '41, Archibald Cox '34, and William Ruckelshaus LL.B. '60 left Nixon's administration together.

67. Donald Regan '40, Secretary of the Treasury

68. Robert Coles '50 (The book was **Dead End School**.)

69. Robin Moore, author of **The Green Berets** and **The French Connection**

70. Roger Sessions '15

71. Richard Bissell, author of "The Pajama Game" and **You Can Always Tell a Harvard Man**

72. Elliot Carter

73. John Lithgow

74. John Rockwell '62

75. **Love Story**

HARVARD IN FICTION

1. John Reed

2. **The Homecoming Game**, by Howard Nemerov '41

3. **Absalom, Absalom!**

4. The class of 1913

5. Sever Hall

6. chocolate eclair

7. **Death in a Tenured Position**, by Amanda Cross

8. "The Christian Roommates," by John Updike '54

9. **Harvard Has a Homicide**, by Timothy Fuller '36

10. Widener Library, reserved for men only in the '50s

11. Spenser, in **Valediction,** by Robert B. Parker

Fiction Answers

12. **The Sound and the Fury**, by William Faulkner

13. Alison Forbes Tipsy Barrett

14. Phillips Brooks House

15. **The Golden Apple**, Part 2 of **The Illuminatus! Trilogy**, by Robert Shea and Robert Anton Wilson

16. Minnesota

17. He folds it into a paper airplane and flies it into the Atlantic off Cape Cod, unopened.

18. Eliot Rosewater

19. A whale-ship

20. He jumped off a bridge with two six-pound flat-irons in his pockets and drowned.

21. **The War Between the Tates**, by Alison Lurie '47

22. **Back Bay**, by William Martin '72

23. Beneath the Old South Church on Boylston and Dartmouth

24. **Of Time and the River**, by Thomas Wolfe

25. **Harvard Has a Homicide**

26. **Faithful Are the Wounds**, by May Sarton

Fiction Answers

27. The class of 1944

28. George finishes in 1947.

29. He drives **up** Quincy Street, past the Faculty Club and the Fogg Art Museum to Memorial Hall, at a time when Quincy Street traffic was already one way in the opposite direction.

30. Eugene Gant, in **Of Time and the River**

31. **The Homecoming Game**

32. The Harvard Police Office is now located at 29 Garden Street, not in the basement of Grays Hall; the plans for the restoration of Memorial Hall tower, which burned in 1956, have yet to be executed; and Derek Bok has not (yet) been named to the U.S. Supreme Court.

33. **The Company**, by former Nixon staffer John Ehrlichman

34. **Gravity's Rainbow**, by Thomas Pynchon

35. Tyrone Slothrop

36. Potrait of a Nude Falling Upon Her Neck in a Wet Bathroom

37. **Catch-22**, by Joseph Heller

38. **Girl With a Zebra**, by Perdita Buchan '62

39. Walter Starbuck, in Kurt Vonnegut's **Jailbird**

Fiction Answers

40. **Windsong**, by Nicholas Gagarin '70

41. **Philosophy 4**, by Owen Wister, AB 1882

42. **The Fume of Poppies**, by Jonathan Kozol '58

43. "President Fights Erection in Harvard Square"

44. Ralph Waldo Emerson

45. John Dos Passos '16, who is mentioned in Weller's novel in passing

46. **Love With a Harvard Accent**

47. The Divinity School tower

48. Gazebo

49. Marvin Myles

50. **Stones of the House**, by Theodore Morrison

51. **The Class**, by Erich Segal

52. In Sever Quad

53. Rona Jaffe '51 (The film was **The Best of Everything**.)

BUILDINGS & GROUNDS

1. Shannon Hall is attached to Vanserg.

2. Half a ton of it was melted down by the Continental Army to make bullets to drive the British out of Boston.

3. Memorial Hall; **The Bostonians**, by Henry James

4. It may be due to the fact that he was so unpopular that the entire student body left school in the middle of his second year to express their dislike of him, or it may be due to the fact that his name was Leonard Hoar.

5. 1. d 4. c
   2. e 5. a
   3. f 6. b

6. In the "Delta," the large triangle of land just west of Memorial Hall

7. In Pusey Library, probably in the Theatre Collection Room. **The Onion** is a metal sculpture by Alexander Calder which sits in front of Pusey.

Buildings & Grounds Answers

8. Quentin Compson, the fictitious Harvard freshman of Faulkner's **The Sound and the Fury**

9. Emerson Hall (The words are: "What Is Man That Thou Art Mindful Of Him.")

10. He instructed the proctors to lay low in their rooms. Deprived of the spectacle of frantic instructors, students soon lost interest in the fires.

11. Temporary barracks for a government naval school held in Pierce Hall, Memorial Hall, and elsewhere on the Harvard campus

12. A commons, or dining hall

13. Fifty years, until 1924

14. Elm beetles killed them in 1910.

15. It was built for 116 pounds less than was budgeted, and when this balance was presented to the General Court, the Court returned the sum to the Corporation "in joyful surprise at their not exceeding the appropriation."

16. d)

17. The college brew-house

18. About ninety years

19. A long, low structure of privies built on the east side of University Hall around 1812 and discreetly hidden behind a grove of pines

Buildings & Grounds Answers

20. The college pig-pen, "where the Corporation's own porkers fought with rats for the commons garbage" and "the hideous clamor of a pig-killing was wont to disturb recitations in University," according to Morison

21. In the Yard opposite the middle of Hollis

22. In Sever Quad

23. Wadsworth House (1727), which served as General Washington's headquarters in 1776

24. University Hall (in the basement), and then Boylston Hall in 1858

25. Registering for school, taking a final exam, donating blood, or researching a book on Harvard trivia (These famous personages appear in the stained glass windows of Memorial Hall.)

26. A. Lawrence Lowell

27. "Emily Dickinson above but pure Mae West below"

28. The "Harvard House," built in 1596 by Thomas Rogers. His thirteenth child, Katherine, lived there from age twelve to twenty-one, when she married Robert Harvard.

29. The villa I Tatti, bequeathed to Harvard by its owner, Bernard Berenson

30. The Kennedy Library; I.M. Pei

Buildings & Grounds Answers

31. The Harvard Branch Railroad, which connected with the Fitchburg Line halfway between Union Square and Porter's Station

32. The Town Creek, which originated about where Holworthy was later built, hit what became Mass. Ave. behind today's Straus Hall and emptied into the Charles in the marshes between what is now Eliot and Winthrop Houses

33. Near Petersham, Massachusetts, seventy miles northwest of Cambridge

34. Outdoors, on the Delta

35. False. Paine Hall is the lecture and concert auditorium on the second and third floors of the building, which is known simply as The Music Building.

36. They are all the same man: Anton Joseph Francis Gerhard Frederick Kamp, who posed at age twenty-four.

37. Yes

38. In the days before central heating, students used to use cannonballs heated in the fireplace to keep the room warm. When it came time to move out in the spring, they dropped the cannonballs out the window.

39. In 2882 (The university took a thousand-year lease from the city of Boston in 1882.)

Buildings & Grounds Answers

40. The fire station between Broadway and Cambridge streets

41. Plans called for workers to remove the stones of Boylston but keep them technically standing by putting them in a wall around the Yard. It was decided not to risk antagonizing the wealthy Boylston family with this bit of trickery, so the interior was rebuilt while the old stone shell remained.

42. Just before the game, Yalies painted "BEAT HARVARD" in bright blue letters on its twelve columns. Sandblasting cost over $1000, and the culprits were expelled.

43. The Mather House tower, which beats William James Hall by 2.75 feet

44. Two large bedpans, one under each rhino, which had been slipped under the shrouds the night before by a couple of students

45. Bessie and Victoria

46. Dumbarton Oaks Research Library and Collection

47. Water free falls from the cooling towers atop the Science Center into an underground basin with a volume two-thirds that of Boston's Symphony Hall. This chilled water plant provides air conditioning for a number of buildings, including the Science Center, Gund Hall, and Emerson Hall.

Buildings & Grounds Answers

48. Kennedy himself chose a site at the Business School in October 1963. Then it was thought that the twelve acres of subway yards north of the Charles—where the Kennedy School of Government and the Charles Square complex now stand—would be ideal, but citizens of Cambridge disagreed.

49. Grays Hall

50. Johnson Gate

51. The Nicholas Longworth Anderson Bridge. Larz Anderson (AB 1888), a former U.S. Ambassador to Japan, gave the bridge in memory of his father, Nicholas (AB 1858). The safest bet would be to call it simply the Anderson Bridge.

ASSESSMENTS OF THE COLLEGE AND ITS MEN

1. Charles Sumner, AB 1830

2. Henry Adams to George Santayana

3. Mark Rothko

4. "They're literate, but they don't read."

5. Benjamin Franklin, who deigned to accept an honorary Master of Arts degree from Harvard thirty-one years later

6. James Agee, AB 1932

7. Edward Dahlberg. Not an alumnus of the college, but a very honest man, he once called himself "the most hated man in American letters"—and that is what a biographer called him.

8. Henry Cabot Lodge

9. William James (He changed his mind later.)

10. George Santayana

Assessments Answers

11. Peter Gomes, Plummer Professor of Christian Morals and Minister of Memorial Church

12. The 1830s

13. Henry Adams

14. Edward Everett

15. James Barnes (1866-1936), at least according to Bartlett's

16. "If any man wishes to be humbled and mortified, let him become President of Harvard College."

17. "You Harvard kids are all alike: starved for attention!"

18. we despise you

19. to go to Harvard and turn left

20. Wallace Stevens

21. Lincoln Kirstein

22. S.I. Hayakawa

23. heaven and hell

HISTORY PART II

1. The compound interest on six pecks of corn was astronomical, so Mr. Mason gave the College Library the scores of four Brahms symphonies.

2. He died after one year.

3. They were unwilling to release their minister, Increase Mather, AB 1656, so he could become president of Harvard.

4. Rogers died of a sudden illness just as the sun was emerging from its eclipse.

5. To translate the Old and New Testaments from English into fair Latin

6. The Collegiate School of Connecticut, later renamed "Yale" at Mather's suggestion

7. Boston was experiencing a smallpox epidemic and students were on break.

8. The building was destroyed by fire.

9. **The Christian Warfare Against the Devill, World, and Flesh**

History II Answers

10. British military guards had been stationed at State Street and cannon pointed at the State House door.

11. A maidservant was "great with child," and President Locke took the blame.

12. Concord, because the college had been taken over by the Provincial Congress to quarter soldiers

13. Eight

14. George Washington, in 1776

15. Defeated General Burgoyne and his troops were supposed to be quartered on the campus until they could be transported to Europe (although they ended up staying elsewhere).

16. John Hancock

17. Phi Beta Kappa, which had been founded at the nation's second oldest college, William and Mary, just five years before

18. The Harvard Medical School, by five years

19. the Immediate Government

20. Amherst

21. Blue

22. Andrew Jackson

23. A mob of one thousand armed Irishmen was rumored to be coming to set fire to

History II Answers

the college library in retaliation for the burning of a Roman Catholic church in Charlestown.

24. Edward Everett

25. a Beethoven symphony played in a saw-mill

26. "If this boy passes the examinations, he will be admitted; and if the white students choose to withdraw, all the income of the College will be devoted to his education."

27. Dr. John W. Webster, class of 1811, had just been hanged for murdering Dr. George Parkman, class of 1809, while both were on the Medical School faculty.

28. "the University at Cambridge"

29. 60,000 (So many people wanted a glimpse that the spectators were brought through in ten-minute shifts.)

30. President Walker was stone deaf

31. They had to attend a minimum of only sixteen weeks of lectures and clinical demonstrations (although they had to wait three years to receive the degree), and they had to be tested orally for ten minutes on each of nine subjects (but had to pass only five).

32. "If you will point out any one who knows more, Mr. Adams, I will appoint him." Adams took the job.

History II Answers

33. He explained how a recent Harvard Medical School graduate who practiced in Quincy had killed three patients in succession by an accidental overdose of sulfate of morphia.

34. three mystics, three skeptics, and three dyspeptics (Actually there were thirty-six students.)

35. "I think the numerous narrative histories of epochs is just a let-off to easy-going students from the studies which require thought."

36. False. Mr. and Mrs. Stanford visited Eliot in 1884 while canvassing a number of college administrators on the logistics of founding a college in their son's memory. In answer to her question, President Eliot told Mrs. Stanford one should not attempt it with an endowment of less than $5,000,000. She looked grave, but after a moment her husband said, "Well, Jane, we could manage that, couldn't we?"

37. They were declared graduates en bloc, went to a basement office in the Yard, paid a black man known as Terry five bucks, and were handed their diplomas.

38. Gas masks for U.S. troops and poison gas for the enemy

SPORTS

1. Robert F. Kennedy

2. They had to lower the boats into the water and then slide down the pilings into the boats like firemen.

3. The catcher's mask

4. Second and third bases

5. "You see I'm at the game, to Yell with Hale."

6. Michael Desaulniers '81

7. It was the first time Harvard players wore numbers. (Coach Percy Haughton had resisted numerals because he liked to confuse opponents in every possible way.)

8. The Harvard crew stopped rowing fifty yards from the finish, so Radcliffe crossed the line first and was declared the winner.

9. $5.29 apiece

Sports Answers

10. A. Lawrence Lowell '77, future president of the college

11. "In your **own** beds by eleven!"

12. Basketball

13. Joseph Kennedy, Sr.

14. Stephen Crane (Harvard won 4-0, with a touchdown and a missed goal.)

15. 12,000 miles. He kept to the Charles because no automobiles were allowed there, except on the bottom, "where I seldom go." The **Crimson** nicknamed him "Charles River Lanman."

16. d)

17. They hired Kelly and Clarkson, the Boston Nationals' "$10,000 Battery," to coach them in secret in the loft over the Brattle Square police station.

18. A huge black weather balloon bearing the letters "MIT" inflated, rose, and exploded in a puff of smoke. The coaches of both teams were indignant, but President Bok called it "a stunning practical joke. I give them full credit."

19. He lost twenty-nine yards in five plays.

20. Endicott "Chub" Peabody '42, who made every All-American team his senior year and later served as Governor of Massachusetts

Sports Answers

21. look for a pivot tooth belonging to Francis J. Lane '36

22. A fencing foil

23. He designed goal-guard pads filled with water-soaked sponges so that the puck stopped dead instead of bouncing away from his goalies.

24. "Barry Wood is playing **putrid** football today." (Harvard had upset West Point 14-13, savaged the Texas Longhorns 35-7, and aced Virginia 19-0 that season, but the score at the Dartmouth game when Husing came up with his line was 6-0 Dartmouth. Soon after, though, Wood connected a beautiful forward pass and drop-kicked an extra point to win the game 7-6. Husing was "permanently" persona non grata for one-and-a-half years after that.)

25. The hop-step-and-jump, the pole vault, the hundred, the quarter-mile, the broad jump, and the high jump

26. 1919

27. The Oregon Ducks, who lost to Harvard 7-6

28. Douglas Fairbanks and Charlie Chaplin

29. repeatedly landing on his head

30. The gym was converted into an underwater sound research lab, and the sonar device for submarine warfare was developed there.

Sports Answers

31. Nine

32. A gray cat

33. Harvard won, 22-7.

34. Instead of passing the ball to a back, he kicked it forward, dodged past his opponent, scooped up the ball, and ran deep into Crimson territory. This was a legal play in those days.

35. The Harvard-Yale boat race, won by Harvard on Lake Winnipesaukee on August 3, 1852

36. He was playing with a plaster cast on his arm, concealed under his jersey and glove.

37. Handsome Dan II, Yale's bulldog mascot, had been kidnapped and with the help of some well-placed hamburger was photographed licking the boots of the John Harvard statue.

38. Archibald MacLeish

39. Percy Haughton, a four-year letterman who had a .340 batting average his senior year

40. Harold Abrahams, the Jewish sprinter portrayed in the film **Chariots of Fire**. He was captain of the Oxford/Cambridge team that won the meet against Harvard/Yale at Wembley two years later.

41. Only one. Although one of the top ten

Sports Answers

in assists in the league, and runner-up for Rookie of the Year, he retired after his first season to go into business on the West Coast.

42. The flying wedge, in which two files of runners lined up diagonally **behind** the quarterback, started running at his signal, and converged into a V as they passed him and he snapped the ball, creating a juggernaut of bodies. It did not win the game for Harvard and was banned at the end of the next season.

43. John Culver (D-Iowa)

44. Ken Miyakawa '29 sat on the varsity bench and interpreted the visitors' chatter and signals.

45. Wrestling

46. True. He set a new school record for assists in a single season (twenty-five) but never scored a goal of his own.

47. Edward Kennedy

48. Centre College, from Danville, Kentucky

49. The "Praying Colonels," because they offered a solemn supplication before every game

50. The central portion of the grandstand burned down in the eighth inning.

51. Crew. Someone offered a cup for an intercollegiate two-mile run the day before

163

Sports Answers

the annual regatta at Saratoga.

52. False. It was coined in the 1930s by sportswriter Caswell Adams of the **New York Herald Tribune**.

53. He said, "Start to work on the new building tomorrow. Good night."

54. she didn't meet Arlington High School this season

55. "They can take the points away, but they can't take away the thrill."

56. In what would be the final out-and-back race between the schools, the Yale boat struck and disabled the Harvard shell, which had reached the stake boat first and was turning. So Yale finished first but Harvard was awarded the race on a foul.

57. Yale won the official contest 2-0. The distraught Harvard team arranged a fun rematch for Thanksgiving Day and bet their jerseys on the outcome. Left fullback John Hersey was one Eli who had to give up his jersey.

58. He captained both Yale and Harvard basketball teams. He had been captain of the Yale team in his senior year (1899) and was captain and coach of Harvard's first official team in 1900-01.

59. While fencing on a raised platform under spotlights before a distinguished audience and panel of judges in evening

Sports Answers

dress, Lane took a vicious lunge at his opponent and split his pants right through to the crotch. (He won his match handily, though.)

60. Since the home team supplied the ball, he had it painted crimson, to match the Harvard jerseys. Harvard was Carlisle's only loss that year, 17-0.

61. McGill University of Montreal, in 1874

62. Leverett Saltonstall '14, later U.S. senator from Massachusetts

63. "In a few minutes they will be joined by Harvard's football players."

64. A one-foot drum with a ten-foot drumstick

65. Harvard and Yale (He swam for Yale in the Marine Corps V-12 program in the summer of 1943.)

66. Four

67. Buckley dashed from first to third directly over the pitcher's mound, but since the rival coach and fans had seen it, Harvard coach Floyd Stahl volunteered immediate restitution.

68. The "John Harvard," a coal-burning steam tender which exploded in 1926

69. Undefeated up to the game, Harvard played Yale to a scoreless tie, and the disgusted players, among them kicker Percy Haughton, vowed not to accept their varsity letters if they did not

165

redeem themselves against Penn the following weekend. Penn won, and no letters were awarded in Cambridge.

70. No glove at all. A Fall River catcher introduced the first catcher's mitt in 1875. (All pitches were underhanded until 1883.)

71. Harvard left New Haven with the score in Yale's favor, but lodged a protest that an Eli shot putter—a transfer student named Roos—had already used up his eligibility. Over the weekend the Yale Board of Athletic Control met and agreed, so Harvard was awarded the meet on Monday by a "Roos."

72. A three-year contract dispute with the Cubs turned out so remuneratively for him that he was able to graduate from both the Law and the Business Schools.

73. As the players picked themselves up, Maxwell blew his whistle and shouted, "Ta-ta-ta-time out, ba-ba-boys, while I get my bla-bla-blue jersey!"

74. Robert T. "Bobby" Jones, Jr. '24, who received a special H for winning the 1923 National Open, was ineligible to play for Harvard because he was already a graduate of Georgia Tech when he came to get his BS degree.

75. One shoe came off in the middle of the race, so he finished with a bare foot.

76. The batter was called out, and a near-riot ensued.

77. lost twenty yards!

Sports Answers

78. Six inches

79. He kicked the ball so hard on a slant that it went only a few feet forward and spun back into the Harvard goal.

80. Delaying his entrance for the weigh-in, he came in wearing an undershirt that had belonged to heavyweight champ Primo Carnera and huge, thick-lensed, hornrimmed glasses. "I was afraid I might be overweight," he said to the coach before a waiting crowd. Removing the glasses, he pretended to grope his way to the scales, where he said, "O, Dear! I am a HAWF pound under." The Syracuse team almost had apoplexy trying to be polite and not laugh. The "poor consumptive" Curtin knocked his concerned opponent off his feet five seconds into the first round.

81. A touch football game between the Harvard and Yale political science departments. The Yale Empiricists beat the Harvard Theorists 14-12. Harvard chairman James Q. Wilson injured a knee stepping where a dog had paused.

82. Jim Thorpe

83. Wrestling, which was not voted a minor sport until 1930

84. He swatted a home run during which the ball slipped through a tiny hole in the center field fence above the Harlem River.

85. Harvey Wood at Chapel Hill and Ar-

Sports Answers

nold Palmer at Wake Forest

86. Yale captain Art McBride "blocked" by bracing himself against the goalpost, which stood right on the goal line in those days.

87. While training with the Navy, he won a track D at Dartmouth and a track P at Princeton, and after the war he won his H at Harvard—which gave him a Ph.D.

88. Moe Berg

89. Number 99, the Yale manager Charlie Yeager

90. He stepped to the line in a plain white shirt lacking any insignia, and won in 9:24.4, setting a new intercollegiate and Harvard record.

91. The gridiron took on lengthwise white stripes and became a checkerboard.

92. When the umpire called Mike Drummey safe in his slide into home, Holy Cross catcher Johnny Allen threw the ball far over the stands in anger and forgot to call time out.

93. Nelson Rockefeller

94. Originally a Harvard man, he found himself in a Blue uniform during military training. Thus, he is the only player to have earned football letters at both Harvard and Yale.

95. he **always** lost the first two games

Sports Answers

96. On Cambridge Common, near the Washington Elm, in 1863

97. Harvard, of course, 29-29

HARVARD IN FILMS

1. **Classmates**

2. Francis X. Bushman, Jr.

3. Yale '16

4. In 1926 the Stadium seated only 38,000. The steel stands added in 1929 raised capacity to 57,750. In any case, we can presume that more than half were Harvard fans.

5. Brek-ek-ek-ex co-ax co-ax
   Brek-ek-ek-ex co-ax co-ax
   O-op O-op Parabalou!
   Yale! Yale! Yale!
   (plundered in part from Aristophanes)

6. **Forever After**

7. Jason Robards

8. **Dirty Tricks**

9. Rudolph Valentino, in 1922's **The Young Rajah**

10. Buster Crabbe

Films Answers

11. Ray Milland

12. Social studies; music

13. Seven

14. **My Man Godfrey**

15. William Powell

16. "He doesn't even belong to the Harvard Club."

17. The Hottentott and the Neanderthal Man

18. Slapsie Maxie Rosenbloom

19. Alan Alda

20. Bob Hope, in **Son of Paleface** (1952)

21. **Dive Bomber** (He's learning how to fly a plane, honest.)

22. He kicks his shoe downfield, which fools everyone while he runs the ball.

23. **Dirty Tricks**, with Elliot Gould and Kate Jackson

24. **H.M. Pulham Esquire** (1940)

25. **The Thomas Crown Affair**

26. "The Bionic Woman" (Lindsay Wagner)

27. **Heaven's Gate**

28. Cambridge, England

Films Answers

29. **Goodbye Columbus**

30. **Manhattan**, with Woody Allen and Diane Keaton

31. **The Bostonians**, with Christopher Reeve and Vanessa Redgrave

32. It's unsanitary.

33. Cecil B. DeMille

34. **Slaughter-House Five**

35. **First Affair**

36. Loretta Swit

37. The University of Washington

38. **HELP**

39. In a story that takes place in the 1880s, the Memorial Hall Tower which burned in 1956 is missing, and a scene at Harvard Hall includes the guardhouse built in 1982.

40. **Altered States**

41. **A Small Circle of Friends**

42. Van Heflin

STUDENT LIFE

1. Yes, for the first twenty years of the college's existence at least, until the first English description of the theories of Copernicus, Galileo, and Kepler was published in 1656

2. "dig"

3. bed

4. A number of them had smashed a tutor's windows, destroyed his furniture, and rung the college bell in the middle of the night; none of the rest would finger the culprits.

5. A hunk of bread and a pot of beer

6. The Helter Skelter Club

7. Required to translate passages of the Hebrew Bible out loud into Greek, they would slip a page of the Greek Old Testament into the official bible to be read.

8. Without skipping a beat, he said, "Good morning, gentlemen."

Student Life Answers

9. 221 years (until 1857)

10. One. The teacher lectured for an hour, the students worked over the subject matter of the lecture for two, they recited during the fourth hour, and then they discussed the material for another two.

11. a testicle

12. In the Parker House bar

13. In what would become known as the "diploma riots," students were protesting the administration's decision to change the language on Harvard diplomas from Latin to English.

14. Hebrew

15. Samuel Adams, AB 1740, James Otis, AB 1743, and John Hancock, AB 1754 (They were all members of the Massachusetts General Court, which was taking refuge at a place "unusual, uncomfortable, and distant" from the depository of public records, as the Declaration of Independence was to put it.)

16. rustication

17. Eating meals "uncovered" (i.e., without a hat)

18. It began at six o'clock in the morning, and lasted the entire day.

19. "The Med. Fac. Society"

Student Life Answers

20. Alexander I, Emperor of Russia

21. cold water (a chancy substance in those days)

22. 270 (according to Morison)

23. a) "Rice Paddies"
    b) "Boats"
    c) "Gas Stations"
    d) "Rumors about Tumors"
    e) "Maps for Saps" and "Palm Trees," respectively
    f) "Darkness at Noon"
    g) "Nuts and Sluts"
    h) "Krauts and Doubts" or "Springterm for Hitler"

24. English

25. Oscar Wilde. When he mounted the stage, he smiled to the Harvard contingent to put them at ease, then said, "I see about me the signs of an aesthetic movement. I see young men who are no doubt sincere, but I can assure them they are no more than caricatures." From then on he had the rest of the audience, uneasy when they had arrived, in the palm of his hand.

26. 1834; they were protesting President Quincy's decision to go outside the university and have the Grand Jury of Middlesex County find and discipline the vandals of question four.

27. Three gallons for degree-takers, one gallon for others

28. One play of Shakespeare's and George Eliot's **Silas Marner** (Actually, things seem to have deteriorated even further in the quarter century since: the author, an English honors graduate, has **yet** to read **Silas Marner**.)

29. Sophomores and freshmen had a classic brawl on the Delta as a hazing ritual on the first Monday of the school year. When the faculty banned it in 1860, students erected a wooden monument which read "Hic jacet Footballum Fightum."

30. A tuition hike from $20 to $25

31. The possession of "any distylled Liquors"

THE WOMEN

1. Helen Keller

2. Lady Mowlson, born Anne Radcliffe, who had given Harvard its very first scholarship: one hundred pounds in 1643

3. Sixty-nine years later, in 1963

4. A ledger in which Radcliffe students recorded the name of any overnight (female) guests so that—theoretically—bodies could be identified in the event of a fire

5. "The Society for the Collegiate Instruction of Women"

6. "The Harvard Annexe"

7. She felt it would be too masculine and would "attract unfavorable comment," and she recommended "pretty, simple dresses." (The class of 1896 was the first to wear caps and gowns.)

8. b)

9. In 1943 coeducation for all but freshmen was instituted as a temporary expedient (which became permanent) because so many men—both students and faculty—had left to join the armed services.

10. Gertrude Stein. William James sent her a postcard the following day which read, "Dear Miss Stein, I understand perfectly how you feel. I often feel like that myself."

11. Prof. Charles Townsend "Copey" Copeland

12. John Kenneth Galbraith

13. 1) She was not to enter the Harvard Club of Boston; 2) she was not to march in the commencement procession; and 3) she was not to ask for the professor's quota of football tickets.

14. "Harvard is not coeducational in theory, only in practice."

15. Women had been borrowing male clothing for the male roles in their play productions. Thereafter, women playing men were required to wear skirts with bloomers underneath.

16. In 1872 he announced in a series of lectures that concentrated academic study would be injurious to the health of young women. The four years corresponding to college age were crucial to the development of a woman's reproductive system, he declared, and

this development would be harmed by allowing energy to be diverted into the mind. His theories were published as **Sex in Education** in 1874.

17. Claudia Weill '69

18. Posture pictures were taken of Radcliffe freshmen in the nude.

19. "... had no Radcliffe maiden
   Who knew mob psychology." (from "Caesar Was a Roman," by Lydia Edwards '27 and Elizabeth Neal '25)

20. "jolly-ups"

21. Maxine Kumin '46

22. Because dormitories were overcrowded with WAVEs, housed at the college to receive instruction at Harvard's Navy Supply Corps School

23. Gertrude Stein

24. Victoria Lincoln '26

25. That they were the only girls in the world to de-emphasize their bosoms and emphasize their feet

26. "Any young lady who has sense enough to take my course deserves an A."

27. Some scientists believed her husband had actually done all the work.

28. Anne McCaffrey '47, author of the Dragonriders of Pern series

Women Answers

29. **Candida**, by George Bernard Shaw

30. False. No men were allowed above the first floor of Radcliffe dorms. Hooks were installed for the purpose of ventilation.

31. Frances FitzGerald

32. Field hockey (Ms. Applebee improvised with men's ice hockey sticks, some field hockey sticks discarded by an Englishman, and a white-painted baseball. A director of physical education at Bryn Mawr for twenty-five years, she lived to the ripe age of 107.)

33. William E. Byerly, who was the first member of the Harvard faculty to agree to teach at the Annexe. Byerly concluded that the demand on a Harvard instructor's time had been "a burden certainly, but not a crushing burden."

34. Talk dirty

35. Ursula K. LeGuin, author of **The Earthsea Trilogy**

36. Rona Jaffe '51 and Warren Beatty

37. Stockard Channing '65, in **The Fortune**

38. Ellen Goodman '63

39. Barbara Tuchman

40. Diana Trilling

41. Alison Lurie '47 (The novel was **Foreign Affairs**.)

SCHOOL DAYS

1. He was hit in the eye by a hard piece of bread during a food fight, though he was not a participant.

2. J.P. Morgan

3. In his junior year he decided to extend his spring break an extra week by going to Bermuda and sending a note to the dean of students explaining that he needed more vacation time. Dean Hurlbut declared, "It is really time for him to go away from Cambridge and note that although he is away the University does not totter."

4. Theodore H. White

5. Bernard Berenson

6. Theodore Roosevelt. "Wine always make me fighty," he remarked.

7. Franklin D. Roosevelt

8. Joseph P. Kennedy; "Mayflower"

School Days Answers

9. Charles Sumner

10. e.e. cummings

11. James Agee

12. Ralph Waldo Emerson

13. Oliver Wendell Holmes, Jr.

14. MIT, which insisted that he spend an additional year in secondary school because he was only sixteen.

15. Aeronautical engineering

16. John F. Kennedy

17. Theodore Roosevelt

18. John Hancock

19. John Quincy Adams

20. Alan Jay Lerner, librettist for **My Fair Lady**, **Gigi**, and **Paint Your Wagon**

21. John Updike

22. Robert F. Kennedy

23. Henry Cabot Lodge, Jr.

24. Francis Parkman

25. Henry Kissinger

26. Owen Wister, author of **The Virginian**

27. T.S. Eliot

School Days Answers

28. Richard Henry Dana, **Two Years Before the Mast**

29. Washington Allston

30. Lucius Beebe

31. Theodore H. White, who screamed the headlines in Latin whenever he saw an old Latin School buddy riding the trolley to BU or MIT

32. W.E.B. DuBois, MA 1891, Ph.D. 1895

33. George Santayana, AB 1886

34. Theodore Roosevelt

35. Edward Kennedy

36. Henry Kissinger

37. Van Wyck Brooks was admitted on probation for earning mostly D's and E's on his entrance exams. He received all C's and D's his freshman year save for one lonely A in an English lit survey course taught by Professors Briggs, Kittredge, and Perry. But he finished in three years and received his key, he once surmised, probably due to the influence of friends.

38. Charles W. Eliot, who joined Alpha Delta Phi and eventually became its president.

39. Bern(h)ard Berenson

40. Samuel Eliot Morison '08

School Days Answers

41. Lincoln Kirstein '30, co-founder of the School of American Ballet with George Balanchine

42. Yo-Yo Ma, age seven, was accompanied by his sister Yeou-Cheng, eleven, with Leonard Berstein '39 conducting.

43. Andre Gregory '56

44. Edward Everett Hale, with the assistance of Samuel Longfellow, younger brother of the poet

45. Washington Allston

46. Conrad Aiken

47. Lucius Beebe

48. Theodore H. White

49. Bernard Berenson

50. **Oh Dad, Poor Dad, Mamma's Hung You in the Closet and I'm Feelin' So Sad**, by Arthur L. Kopit

51. The nine Beethoven symphonies (on 78s!)

52. George Santayana

53. It was narrowly defeated, 1,324 to 1,227.

54. T.S. Eliot

55. Lincoln Kirstein

56. Cotton Mather, AB 1678

School Days Answers

57. John Hawkes

58. Jack Lemmon

59. Virgil Thomson

60. Arthur L. Kopit '59

61. Chris Wallace

62. Robert E. Sherwood, author of **The Petrified Forest**, **Abe Lincoln in Illinois**, and the screenplays for Hitchcock's **Rebecca** and Wyler's **The Best Years of Our Lives**

63. it was written in Boolean algebra

64. Increase Mather, sixth president of Harvard and father of Cotton

65. John Hawkes '49, who was soon discharged from the army on account of his asthma, but made it to Europe as an ambulance driver

66. entomologist

67. Cotton Mather, who entered at age eleven-and-a-half. His father had enrolled at the hoary age of twelve.

68. Malcolm Cowley

69. J. Robert Oppenheimer

70. Hal Clement, author of **Needle**, **Iceworld**, and **Mission of Gravity**

71. Philip Johnson '27

School Days Answers

72. Christopher Lasch '54, author of **The Culture of Narcissism**

73. John Green, the five-time Oscar winner known as "Mr. M-G-M Music"

74. Walter Lippmann '10

DROPOUTS & SPECIAL STUDENTS

1. Pete Seeger

2. R. Buckminster Fuller

3. William Randolph Hearst

4. Wallace Stevens

5. Howard Hughes, Sr.

6. While preparing infant formula, he spilled the milk down a well. Fearing the spread of typhoid germs, he went down into the well barefoot to empty it out. Not feeling too badly the next day, he went clamming.

7. Edwin Arlington Robinson

8. Eugene O'Neill

9. Polaroid's Edwin Land

10. Bonnie Raitt

11. Ogden Nash

Dropouts & Special Students Answers

12. Gram Parsons, who later joined the Byrds and the Flying Burrito Brothers

13. To celebrate the victory of Cleveland over Blaine in 1884, he and some friends released a flock of roosters in the Yard during the night so that a raucous chorus of crowing greeted the residents at dawn. Hearst and Co. were also responsible for some property damage on that occasion.

14. Eugene O'Neill

15. Wallace Stevens (The highest offer he received was $35.)

16. Gram Parsons

17. Alfred Alistair Cooke

18. His junior year he sent each of his instructors a large package which contained a chamber pot with the recipient's name ornamentally lettered on the inside bottom.

19. William Ellery Channing II

20. "Triflecut College"

21. During his visit to the United States in 1920-21, he registered in a Harvard course called "English E," an English language class for foreign students.

22. Gram Parsons

23. He couldn't get permission to leave school to compete in the first modern

Dropouts & Special Students Answers

Olympic Games in 1896. He went anyway, wore a suit sewn by his mom, and brought home the first U.S. gold medal in modern Olympic history—in the first final in the modern Games, the hop-step-and-jump. He also took a silver medal in the high jump.

24. Robert Lowell

PHOTOGRAPHS

1. John Harvard
2. "The Statue of the Three Lies"
3. Sherman Hoar, class of 1882
4. The Statue of Liberty, the Lincoln Memorial, and the Ben Franklin statue in Philadelphia
5. To shelter University guards
6. $57,000, or about $1,000 per square foot
7. Widener Library
8. Houghton Library
9. Pusey
10. When Eleanor Elkins Widener donated the money for a library in the memory of her son Harry (AB 1907), the bequest stipulated that not one brick could be moved once the building was erected. In order to build a connector between Widener and Houghton libraries, an

Photos Answers

elevated passage through a window frame of Widener had to be constructed.

11. Gore Hall

12. The college library

13. Widener Library

14. One of the buildings of Winthrop House

15. Wadsworth House

16. Grays Hall

17. Holyoke Center (10th floor terrace)

18. Hicks House

19. Wood Street until 1838, Brighton Street until 1882, Boylston Street until 1982, and John F. Kennedy Street since then

20. John Hicks was killed on April 20, 1776, near Porter's Station while harrassing the British retreat from Lexington.

21. It is the Kirkland House library.

22. Hemenway Gymnasium

23. Three

24. Littauer Center

25. Charlestown

26. Edward Everett, president of Harvard 1846-1849

Photos Answers

27. The Arthur M. Sackler Museum

28. Burr Hall

29. Everyone's entitled to his own opinion.

30. Memorial Church

31. Sever Hall

32. Emerson Hall

33. The Carpenter Center for the Visual Arts

34. Brother Blue

35. Hugh Morgan Hill

36. 1948

37. Deer Island Prison

38. the Fogg Art Museum

39. Hunt Hall and Robinson Annexe

40. Canaday Hall

41. Holden Chapel

42. The western end

43. Lionel Hall

44. Harvard Hall

45. Charlestown

46. The home and land of John Harvard

Photos Answers

47. Richard Henry Dana

48. astronomical observatory

49. Lamont Library

50. Dana-Palmer House

51. Mallinckrodt

52. Chemistry

53. As a train station for the Harvard Branch Railroad

54. As a dining hall known as Thayer Commons

55. Austin Hall

56. The Rev. Peter Gomes

57. Lowell Lecture Hall

58. Absolutely nothing, aside from storage

59. Kirkland Street

60. The Busch-Reisinger Museum

61. The Harvard Advocate Building

62. South Street

63. Bow Street, across from the **Lampoon**

64. They had published "Glittering Pie," a story by Henry Miller replete with blanks.

65. The Harvard-Yenching Library

Photos Answers

66. The Semitic Museum

67. The Biological Labs

68. Divinity Avenue

69. Riesman Center-Hillel House

70. The Fly Club

71. Holyoke Place

72. Lowell, Quincy, and Leverett

73. Dane Hall

74. The Law School

75. President's office

76. Grays Hall

77. Lehman Hall

MISCELLANY

1. False. It is the oldest in the United States, but the Spanish had founded universities in Mexico City, Lima, and Cordoba (Argentina) before the Pilgrims landed.

2. Richard Alpert and Timothy Leary

3. "Rinehart!"

4. Four pieces of printing type from the Cambridge press (one of which was used in the publication of John Eliot's **The Indian Grammar** in 1666)

5. Pogo, the Okefenokee possum

6. Piazzo Leprechauno

7. A cooperative venture in which students led courses—on such topics as Norman Mailer, Bob Dylan, the History of the Self, and Motorcycles and Sex—during the 1969 student strike

8. Warren G. Harding

Miscellany Answers

9. "And there may be many others but they haven't been dis-cah-vered." (from Tom Lehrer's "The Elements")

10. A. Lawrence Lowell, whose sister was Amy Lowell

11. Edward Everett Hale and Nathan Hale, respectively

12. e) Quincy Adams Wagstaff is the name of the president of Huxley College played by Groucho Marx in the film **Horsefeathers**.

13. **The Necronomicon**, by the mad Arab poet Abdul Alhazred

14. "The President is in Washington to see Mr. Wilson."

15. The Beatles album "Sgt. Pepper's Lonely Hearts Club Band"

16. Harvard gave it up, and it became a leper colony.

17. "Minute Rice"

18. He went to a Caribbean island for three weeks with no companions except Samuel Eliot Morison's histories of Harvard and three gallons of rum.

19. Ernie Pyle was killed in the Pacific theater between the time of his selection and commencement.

20. "They are a set of naturals from that insane asylum near Boston. Their keeper just told me so."

Miscellany Answers

21. St. Grottlesex

22. i)

23. John Barleycorn

24. W. Somerset Maugham

25. a)

26. The Marquis de Lafayette

27. President Pusey wanted to call him the "sidewalk superintendent of our times" in the citation, and Classics Professor Mason Hammond couldn't find a Latin equivalent for the phrase.

28. Eight (The Boston School Committee had initiated a short-lived experiment establishing a two-year preparatory course to precede the traditional six-year program, so Santayana entered Boston Latin at age ten.)

29. "Of course there isn't any, but it will do him good to find it out!" (And it did, too, says Morison.)

30. As of fiscal year 1984, $21.86 (up from a low of $11.90 in 1970!)

31. Horse steak

32. It was taken off most recently in 1983 because the chef hated it.

33. I-c, II-a, III-a, IV-b

Miscellany Answers

34. Back when it was a Delta Phi chapter, James Gore King '89 and J.P. Morgan '89 procured land, built a clubhouse, and kept every room brilliantly illuminated to give the impression that this was where the action was on campus.

35. Gardening (The soil was so rocky that a garden almost had to be hewn out of the land.)

36. That it was a peculiarly low form of cunning

37. Grover Cleveland

38. John Simon Guggenheim Memorial Foundation

39. "Oh, oh! So overdone! So Renaissance!" The joke went on to say he ended up settling for Heaven when he learned that in Hell he would have to live in view of Appleton Chapel.

40. Kittredge (George Lyman Kittredge had bothered only to earn an AB, but that didn't prevent him from becoming a world authority on Shakespeare and teaching at Harvard for forty-eight years. When someone asked why he hadn't taken a Ph.D. he replied, "Who would have examined me?")

41. Peter Benchley, James Agee, Michael Crichton, and Robert E. Sherwood, respectively

42. He wrote a play "of the Elizabethan type"—a five-volume, five-part drama entitled **Elizabeth of England**, which

ran to 800 pages in length. (He also published 300 pages of poems of the Civil War, **From Old Fields**.)

43. Barrett Wendell, whose book **The France of Today** delighted the French —although Santayana said Wendell's books were not worth writing

44. P.D.Q. Bach (1807-1742?)

45. The Magnolia Gardens in Charleston, South Carolina. Its "John Harvard," perhaps the only extant specimen in the world, has a trunk four feet in circumference and thirty-six feet in height.

46. The peony. Its "John Harvard" was developed by Edward Auten '04.

47. Eggs McMuffin

48. Leon Trotsky

49. icebox

50. Drawings and paintings by these literary masters are kept in the Fogg Museum.

51. The bill resolved that "no one shall hereafter be convicted of a crime of murdering any Harvard graduate, Rhodes scholar or student, except upon testimony of the deceased in open court." This worthy measure apparently was not taken up at the next legislative session.

52. John D. MacDonald, author of the Travis McGee series

Miscellany Answers

53. Stock options

54. Paul Myron Anthony Linebarger—who spoke Chinese, German, French and Spanish; who could read Russian, Portuguese and Dutch; who served as his father's secretary at age seventeen when the latter was a legal advisor to Sun Yat Sen; who attended the University of Nanking, George Washington University, Oxford, Chicago and Johns Hopkins; who had a certificate in psychiatry; and who wrote unique science fiction under the pseudonym "Cordwainer Smith"—taught at Harvard in 1936-37.

55. Professor Alfred Harbage, expert on 16th-century English drama and editor of the Pelican Shakespeare

56. First- and second-chair lawnmower, chain saws, and a percussion section consisting of a baseball bat and garbage can, and a cap gun. The performance was billed as the Lawn Care Equipment Concert.

57. "What's pat in Latin, and chic in Greek, I always distinguish more easily in English."

58. Picasso's **Guernica**, the appearance of which prompted the headline in a Boston newspaper, "Phantasmagoria or Just Plain Nuts: Harvard Division Over Picasso"

59. There is none. The correct name is **Quercus havardii**, for the little tree was named after V. Havard, who collected it in 1853.

Miscellany Answers

60. Burn it

61. Under the most rigorously controlled conditions of pressure, temperature, volume, humidity, and other variables, the organism will do as it damn well pleases.

62. The 1985 bill was only $12,000 because alumni are turning from hard liquor to light wines, beer, and Perrier. "On a hot day we serve a lot of gin and tonics, vodka and tonics, and Bloody Marys," says reunion director Marion Briefer, "but bourbon and scotch are practically untouched."

63. woolly mammoths

Which of the following trivial facts about David Loftus is true?

- a) He was born and raised in Oregon.
- b) He finished his undergraduate thesis four days before it was due.
- c) He once appeared on stage with Estelle Parsons.
- d) He is a member of the Black Jokers morris team.
- e) He has read **Ulysses** twice but failed twice to finish both **Remembrance of Things Past** and **Gravity's Rainbow**.
- f) He has never attended a Harvard football game.
- g) He is a fan of Fats Waller, Gentle Giant, Bartok, Spike Jones, and the Roches.
- h) He lived in Hanau, West Germany for two years.
- i) He has tape recorded for the use of the blind **Confederacy of Dunces**, **The Origin of Consciousness in the Breakdown of the Bicameral Mind**, **The Happy Hustler**, and a walking tour of the Boston University campus.
- j) He collects books by John Fowles and Harlan Ellison.
- k) In Louisiana during the summer of 1978, he was knifed and he spent a day in jail.
- l) He is a great writer of letters and plans one day to write an unauthorized autobiography.
- m) He is an insufferable prig and has no sense of humor.
- n) All of the above